The Dirty Bits

The
Dirty Bits

collected and introduced by
Lesley Cunliffe, Craig Brown
and Jon Connell

ANDRE DEUTSCH

First published 1981 by
André Deutsch Limited
105 Great Russell Street London WC1

Copyright © 1981 by Craig Brown,
Lesley Cunliffe and Jon Connell
All rights reserved

Printed in Great Britain by
The Thetford Press Limited
Thetford Norfolk

ISBN 0 233 97395 8

Contents

ACKNOWLEDGEMENTS

The authors and publishers would like to acknowledge the kind permission of the following for use of extracts: The Bodley Head: Jules Romains, *The Body's Rapture* trans. John Rodker; The Catholic University of America Press: Clement of Alexandria, 'Christ the Educator', vol. 23, *Fathers of the Church* trans. Simon P. Wood; Early English Text Society: *The Exeter Book* trans. W.S. Mackie; Faber & Faber: Petronius, *The Satyricon and The Fragments* trans. John Sullivan; Robert Graves: Apuleius, *The Golden Ass*; The Loeb Classical Library (William Heinemann): Apuleius, *The Golden Ass* trans. W. Adlington, Aristotle, *Generation of Animals* trans. A.L. Peck, Plato, *Symposium* trans. H. Rackham and Pliny, *Natural History* trans. W.H.S. Jones; Penguin Books: St Augustine, *Confessions* trans. R.S. Pine-Coffin, *Epic of Gilgamesh* trans. N.K. Sandars, Juvenal, *Sixteen Satires* trans. Peter Green; Choderlos Laclos, *Les Liaisons Dangereuses* trans. P.W.K. Stone, Rousseau, *The Confessions* trans. J.H. Cohen, Voltaire, *Candide* trans. John Butt and Zola, *Nana* trans. George Holden; Secker & Warburg: Thomas Mann, *Holy Sinner* trans. H.T. Lowe-Porter and Robert Musil, *Young Törless* trans. Kaiser and Williams; The Society of Authors as agents for the Strachey Trust: Lytton Strachey, *Ermyntrude and Esmerelda*; Michael Yeats, Anne Yeats and Macmillan London Limited: W.B. Yeats, 'The Stick of Incense'.

They would also like to acknowledge the kind permission of the following for reproduction of illustrations: *Ashmolean Museum*: p. 107; *Andrew Edmunds*: James Gillray p. 143; *Guildhall Library*: Thomas Rowlandson pp. 9 and 131; *The Mansell Collection*: pp. 46, 53 and 74; *Mary Evans Picture Library*: Gell p. 2, Moreau p. 38, Félicien Rops p. 69, Aubrey Beardsley p. 82, Thomas Rowlandson p. 135, and pp. iii, 18, 25, 33, 88, 94 and 140; *Victoria and Albert Museum (Crown Copyright)*: Simon Petit p. 116, and pp. 61 and 124.

The copy on the endpapers is reproduced from the *Oxford English Dictionary* and from the *Concise Oxford Dictionary*, by permission of Oxford University Press.

Introduction

Here at last, bound in one volume, are all those extracts from the classics that sully the good name of literature. Now that they have been caged between two covers they can no longer strike at the very heart, and beyond, of the diligent youngster. Never again will self-improvement be turned to abuse, for with the aid of *The Dirty Bits* each parent will be able to tell, at a glance, just which books, masquerading as respectable, even beneficial, are in fact the works of minds bent on perversion.

Commendable though some of its passages may be, the Bible is just such a book. Crammed to its very brink with lechery, harlotry, sodomy and adultery (all of them bravely exposed in this volume) the self-styled Good Book can now be seen as the foundation stone for the bordello of licentiousness and depravity that is so often, and so misleadingly, termed 'Improving Literature. It is no secret that the Works of William Shakespeare, oozing as they are with rampant homosexuality, transvestism and incest (examples of each contained herein), are freely available at many centres of learning, their perusal encouraged by those intent on broadening the minds, and much else besides, of the young and impressionable. The same is true of Charlotte Bronte and Herman Melville, whose blatant descriptions of vice (extracted and collected here for the first time) are amongst the most fulsome, offering grave temptation to any innocent mind intent on mischief.

The conscientious parent or guardian will feel gratitude for the service this book provides. To steady the roving eye or the prying hand has long been the prime duty of the adult within the community, but up until now there has been no true guide as to where lust lies in literature. The back would be turned, the description of what Lot's daughters got up to with their father would be all but read. How could the caring parent or guardian know which books to propagate and which to hide away? To the sound of sighs up and down the nation, *The Dirty Bits* presents the answer.

It is with confidence that we suggest that the Lord was on our side throughout this enterprise, for what else could explain the way in which so many books — *The Compleat Angler*, *Martin Chuzzlewit* and many others — would miraculously fall open at their most disgraceful passages the moment they were taken off the library shelves? And surely it was God's prompting that conjured up in the mouths of some of Britain's most respected men of letters verbatim quotations from the lewdest literature in the world.

We are deeply grateful to all the honest folk who took time to search out and lay bare the Dirty Bits in literature which had troubled their childhood minds: Professor Sir Kenneth Dover, Stephen Medcalf, Professor Tony Nuttall, Rupert and Anya Forbes Adam, Melvyn Bragg, Richard Boston, John Gross, Mary Killen, Frank Muir, Richard Hoggart, Graham Bradshaw and, finally, the late Ivy Litvinov, to whom this book is dedicated.

Lesley Cunliffe
Craig Brown
Jon Connell

Prologue

His classic studies made a little puzzle,
   Because of filthy loves of gods and goddesses,
Who in the earlier ages raised a bustle,
   But never put on pantaloons or boddices.
His reverend tutors had at times a tussle,
   And for their Æneids, Iliads, and Odysseys,
Were forced to make an odd sort of apology,
For Donna Inez dreaded the mythology.

Ovid's a rake, as half his verses show him,
   Anacreon's morals are a still worse sample,
Catullus scarcely had a decent poem,
   I don't think Sappho's Ode a good example,
Although Longinus tells us there is no hymn
   Where the sublime soars forth on wings more ample;
But Virgil's songs are pure, except that horrid one
Beginning with 'Formosum Pastor Corydon.'

Lucretius' irreligion is too strong
   For early stomachs to prove wholesome food;
I can't help thinking Juvenal was wrong,
   Although no doubt his real intent was good,
For speaking out so plainly in his song,
   So much, indeed, as to be downright rude;
And then what proper person can be partial
To all those nauseous epigrams of Martial?

Juan was taught from out the best edition,
  Expurgated by learned men, who place,
Judiciously, from out the schoolboy's vision,
  The grosser parts; but fearful to deface
Too much their modest bard by this omission,
  And pitying sore his mutilated case,
They only add them all in an appendix,
Which saves in fact the trouble of an index:

For there we have them all at one fell swoop,
  Instead of being scatter'd through the pages;
They stand forth marshall'd in a handsome troop,
  To meet the ingenuous youth of future ages,
Till some less rigid editor shall stoop
  To call them back into their separate cages,
Instead of standing staring all together,
Like garden-gods — and not so decent either.

Lord Byron from *Don Juan* (XLI — XLV)

Dreaming Spires

Wrætlic hongað   bi weres þeo
frean under sceate   foran is þyrel
bið stiþ ond heard   stede hafað godne
þonne se esne   his agen hrægl
ofer cneo hefeð   wile þæt cuþe hol
mid his hangellan   heafde gretan
þæt he efelang ær   oft gefylde:

A strange thing hangs by a man's thigh
under its master's clothes. It is pierced in front
is stiff and hard, has a good fixed place.
When the man lifts his own garment
up above his knee, he wishes to visit
with the head of this hanging instrument the familiar hole
which it, when of equal length, has often filled before.

(probable answer: key)   from *The Exeter Book of Riddles* c 975
                                           translated by W.S. Mackie

✿

The infant giant's women attendants are playing with him.

One of them would call it her little dille, her staff of love, her
quillety, her faucetin, her dandilollie: Another her peen, her
jolly kyle, her bableret, her membretoon, her quickset imp:
Another again, her branch of coral, her female adamant, her

3

placket-racket, her Cyprian sceptre, her jewel for ladies: and some of the women would give it these names, my bunguetee, my stopple too, my busherusher, my gallant wimble, my pretty boarer, my coney-burrow ferret, my little piercer, my augretine, my dangling hangers, down right to it, stiff and stout, in and to, my pusher, dresser, pouting stick, my honey pipe, my pretty pillicock, linkie pinkie, futilletie, my lusty andouille and crimson chitterlin, my little couille bredouille, my pretty rogue, and so forth. . .

Rabelais from *Gargantua and Pantagruel*
translated by Sir Thomas Urquhart

O folk, I have a wondrous tale, so rare
Much shall it profit hearers wise and ware!
I saw in salad years a potent Brave
And sharp of edge and point his warrior glaive;
Who entered joust and list with hardiment
Fearless of risk, of victory confident,
His vigorous onset straitest places oped
And easy passage through all narrows groped.

*   *   *   *   *

Thuswise full many a night his part he played
In strength and youthtide's stately garb arrayed,
Dealing to fair young girl delicious joy
And no less welcome to the blooming boy.
But Time ne'er ceased to stint his wondrous strength
(Steadfast and upright as the gallow's length)
Until the Nights o'erthrew him by their might
And friends condemned him for a feckless wight;

Nor was a wizard but who wasted skill
Over his case, nor leach could heal his ill.
Then he abandoned arms abandoned him
Who gave and took salutes so fierce and grim;
And now lies prostrate drooping haughty crest;
For who lives longest him most ills molest.
Then see him, here he lies on bier for bed: —
Who will a shroud bestow on stranger dead?

translated from the Arabic by Sir Richard Burton

✺

... have we some strange Indian with the great tool come to court, the women so besiege us? Bless me, what a fry of fornication is at door!

William Shakespeare from *Henry VIII*

✺

Had you stepped on board the Pequod at a certain juncture of this post-mortemizing of the whale; and had you strolled forward nigh the windlass, pretty sure am I that you would have scanned with no small curiosity a very strange, enigmatical object,* which you would have seen there, lying along lengthwise in the lee scuppers. Not the wondrous cistern in the whale's huge head; not the prodigy of his unhinged lower jaw; not the miracle of his symmetrical tail; none of these would so surprise you, as half a glimpse of that unaccountable cone, — longer than a Kentuckian

*The whale's penis

5

is tall, nigh a foot in diameter at the base, and jet-black as Yojo, the ebony idol of Queequeg. And an idol, indeed, it is; or, rather, in old times, its likeness was. Such an idol as that found in the secret groves of Queen Maachah in Judea; and for worshipping which, King Asa, her son, did depose her, and destroyed the idol, and burnt it for an abomination at the brook Kedron, as darkly set forth in the fifteenth chapter of the first book of Kings.

Look at the sailor, called the mincer, who now comes along, and assisted by two allies, heavily backs the grandissimus, as the mariners call it, and with bowed shoulders, staggers off with it as if he were a grenadier carrying a dead comrade from the field. Extending it upon the forecastle deck, he now proceeds cylindrically to remove its dark pelt, as an African hunter the pelt of a boa. This done he turns the pelt inside out, like a pantaloon leg; gives it a good stretching, so as almost to double its diameter; and at last hangs it, well spread, in the rigging, to dry. Ere long, it is taken down; when removing some three feet of it, towards the pointed extremity, and then cutting two slits for arm-holes at the other end, he lengthwise slips himself bodily into it. The mincer now stands before you invested in the full canonicals of his calling. Immemorial to all his order, this investiture alone will adequately protect him, while employed in the peculiar functions of his office.

That office consists in mincing the horse-pieces of blubber for the pots; an operation which is conducted at a curious wooden horse, planted endwise against the bulwarks, and with a capacious tub beneath it, into which the minced pieces drop, fast as the sheets from a rapt orator's desk. Arrayed in decent black; occupying a conspicuous pulpit; intent on bible leaves; what a candidate for an archbishoprick, what a lad for Pope were this mincer!

Herman Melville from Moby Dick

In the meanwhile, during my sixteenth year, the narrow means of my family obliged me to leave school and live idly at home with my parents. The brambles of lust grew high above my head and there was no one to root them out, certainly not my father. One day at the public baths he saw the signs of active virility coming to life in me and this was enough to make him relish the thought of having grandchildren.

St Augustine from *Confessions*
translated by R. S. Pine-Coffin

∞

15 Know ye not that your bodies are the members of Christ? shall I then take the members of Christ, and make them the members of an harlot? God forbid.
16 What? know ye not that he which is joined to an harlot is one body? for two, saith he, shall be one flesh.

1 Corinthians 6

∞

In this plight they were perishing away, when Zeus in his pity provided a fresh device. He moved their privy parts to the front — for until then they had these, like all else, on the outside, and did their begetting and bringing forth not on each other but on the earth, like the crickets. These parts he now shifted to the front, to be used for propagating on each other — in the female member by means of the male; so that if in their embracements a man should happen on a woman there might be conception and

7

continuation of their kind; and also, if male met with male they might have some satiety of their union and a relief, and so might turn their hands to their labours and their interest to ordinary life.

Plato from *Symposium*
translated by H. Rackham

✲

Trinc, trinc; by Bacchus, let us tope,
And tope again; for, now I hope
To see some brawny, juicy rump
Well tickled with my carnal stump.
Ere long, my friends, I shall be wedded,
Sure as my trap-stick has a red-head;
And my sweet wife shall hold the combat
Long as my baws can on her bum beat.

Rabelais from *Gargantua and Pantagruel*
translated by Sir Thomas Urquhart

✲

'Say! You, who are up to fighting a man with your bare hands, could you — eh? — could you manage to stick one with a thing like that knife of mine?'

She opened her eyes very wide and gave him a wild smile.

'How can I tell?' she whispered enchantingly. 'Will you let me have a look at it?'

Without taking his eyes from her face, he pulled the knife out of its sheath — a short, broad, cruel, double-edged blade with a bone handle — and only then looked down at it.

8

Rowlandson Del

'A good friend,' he said simply. 'Take it in your hand and feel the balance,' he suggested.

At the moment when she bent forward to receive it from him, there was a flash of fire in her mysterious eyes — a red gleam in the white mist which wrapped the promptings and longings of her soul. She had done it! The very sting of death was in her hands; the venom of the viper in her paradise, extracted, safe in her possession — and its head all but lying under her heel. Ricardo, stretched on the mats of the floor, crept closer and closer to the chair in which she sat.

All her thoughts were busy planning how to keep possession of that weapon which had seemed to have drawn into itself every danger and menace on the death-ridden earth. She said with a low laugh, the exultation in which he failed to recognise:

'I didn't think that you would ever trust me with that thing!'

*   *   *   *   *

The knife was lying in her lap. She let it slip into the fold of her dress, and laid her forearms with clasped fingers over her knees, which she pressed desperately together. The dreaded thing was out of sight at last. She felt a dampness break out all over her.

Joseph Conrad from *Victory*

King Arthur encounters a giant.

... he shappis at sir Arthure, but the kynge shuntys a lytyll and rechis hym a dynte hyghe uppon the haunche, and there he swappis his genytrottys [genitals] in sondir.

Than he rored and brayed and yet angurly he strykes, and fayled of sir Arthure and the erthe hittis, that he kutte into the swarffe a large swerde-length and more. Than the kynge sterte

up unto hym and raught hym a buffette and kut his baly in
sundir, that oute wente the gore, that the grasse and the grounde
all foule was begone.

Sir Thomas Malory from *Le Morte d'Arthur*

෩

Found amid the sphagnum on the dry bank on the south side of
the Turnpike, just below Everett's meadow, a rare and
remarkable fungus, such as I have heard of but never seen
before. The whole height six and three quarters inches, two
thirds of it being buried in the sphagnum. It may be divided into
three parts, pileus, stem, and base, — or scrotum, for it is a
perfect phallus. One of those fungi named *impudicus*, I think. In
all respects a most disgusting object, yet very suggestive. It is
hollow from top to bottom, the form of the hollow answering to
that of the outside. The color of the outside white excepting the
pileus, which is olive-colored and somewhat coarsely corrugated,
with an oblong mouth at tip about one eighth of an inch long, or,
measuring the white lips, half an inch. This cap is thin and white
within, about one and three eighths inches high by one and a
half wide. The stem (bare portion) is three inches long
horizontally viewed of an oval form. Longest diameter at base
one and a half inches, at top (on edge of pileus) fifteen sixteenths
of an inch. Short diameters in both cases about two thirds as
much. It is a delicate white cylinder of a finely honeycombed and
crispy material about three sixteenths of an inch thick, or more,
the whole very straight and regular. The base, or scrotum, is of
an irregular bag form, about one inch by two in the extremes,
consisting of a thick trembling gelatinous mass surrounding the
bottom of the stem and covered with a tough white skin of a
darker tint than the stem. The whole plant rather frail and
trembling. There was at first a very thin delicate white collar (or
volva?) about the base of the stem above the scrotum. It was as
offensive to the eye as to the scent, the cap rapidly melting and

defiling what it touched with a fetid, olivaceous, semiliquid matter.

* * * * *

Pray, what was Nature thinking of when she made this? She almost puts herself on a level with those who draw in privies.

Henry David Thoreau from *Journals*

My agitation became so strong that, being unable to satisfy my desires, I excited them by the most extravagant behaviour. I haunted dark alleys and hidden retreats, where I might be able to expose myself to women in the condition in which I should have liked to have been in their company. What they saw was not an obscene object, I never even thought of such a thing; it was a ridiculous object. The foolish pleasure I took in displaying it before their eyes cannot be described. There was only one step further necessary for me to take, in order to gain actual experience of the treatment I desired, and I have no doubt that some woman would have been bold enough to afford me the amusement, while passing by, if I had had the courage to wait. This folly of mine led to a disaster almost as comical, but less agreeable for myself.

One day, I took up my position at the bottom of a court where there was a well, from which the girls of the house were in the habit of fetching water. At this spot there was a slight descent which led to some cellars by several entrances. In the dark I examined these underground passages, and finding them long and dark, I concluded that there was no outlet, and that, if I happened to be seen and surprised, I should find a safe hiding-place in them. Thus emboldened, I exhibited to the girls who came to the well a sight more laughable than seductive. The

more modest pretended to see nothing; others began to laugh;
others felt insulted and cried out.

> Jean-Jacques Rousseau from *Confessions*
> translated by J.M. Cohen

❧

Wednesday 21 January 1801.   I dined at Deane yesterday, as I
told you I should; — & met the two Mr. Holders. — We played at
Vingt-un, which as Fulwar was unsuccessful, gave him an
opportunity of exposing himself as usual.

> Jane Austen in a letter to her sister, Cassandra

❧

IC on wincle gefrægn   weax[an] nathwæt
ꝥindan *ond* ꝥunian   ꝥecene hebban
on ꝥæt banlease   bryd grapode
hygewlonc hondum   hrægle ꝥeahte
ꝥrintende ꝥing   ꝥeodnes dohtor:

I have heard of something growing in a corner,
swelling and standing up, raising its covering.
At that boneless thing a proud-hearted bride
grasped with her hands; a prince's daughter
covered that swelling thing with her robe.

(probable answer: dough)

> from *The Exeter Book of Riddles c* 975
> translated by W. S. Mackie

13

It must be acknowledged that, asleep or awake, Tom's position in reference to this young lady was full of uneasiness. The more he saw of her, the more he admired her beauty, her intelligence, the amiable qualities that even won on the divided house of Pecksniff, and in a few days restored at all events the semblance of harmony and kindness between the angry sisters. When she spoke, Tom held his breath, so eagerly he listened; when she sang, he sat like one entranced. She touched his organ, and from that bright epoch, even it, the old companion of his happiest hours, incapable as he had thought of elevation, began a new and deified existence.

Charles Dickens from *Martin Chuzzlewit*

There was a young man and a maid fell in love,
Terry derry ding, terry derry ding, terry derry dino.
To get her good will he often did —
Terry derry ding, terry derry ding, langtido dille.
There's many will say, and most will allow,
Terry derry ding, terry derry ding, &c.,
There's nothing so good as a terry derry ding, &c.
I would wish all maids before they be sick,
Terry, derry, &c.
To inquire for a young man that has a good —
Terry derry, &c.

Thomas Heywood from *The Rape of Lucrece*

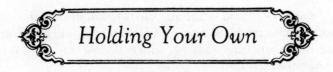

Holding Your Own

8 And Judah said unto Onan, Go in unto thy brother's wife, and marry her, and raise up seed to thy brother.
9 And Onan knew that the seed should not be his; and it came to pass, when he went in unto his brother's wife, that he spilled it on the ground, lest that he should give seed to his brother.
10 And the thing which he did displeased the LORD: wherefore he slew him also.

Genesis 38

It was now my turn to ask the old French officer, 'What was the matter?' for a cry of '*Haussez les mains, Monsieur l'Abbé!*' re-echoed from a dozen different parts of the *parterre*, was as unintelligible to me as my apostrophe to the monk had been to him.

He told me it was some poor Abbé in one of the upper *loges*, who he supposed had got planted *perdu* behind a couple of *grisettes*, in order to see the opera, and that the *parterre*, espying him, were insisting upon his holding up both his hands during the representation — And can it be supposed, said I, that an ecclesiastic would pick the *grisettes'* pockets? — The old French officer smiled, and, whispering in my ear, opened a door of knowledge which I had no idea of.

15

... Good God, said I, turning pale with astonishment, — is it possible that a people so smit with sentiment should at the same time be so unclean, and so unlike themselves? — *Quelle grossierté!* added I.

Laurence Sterne from A *Sentimental Journey*

24 September 1663 In the afternoon, telling my wife that I go to Deptford, I went by water to Westminster Hall; and there finding Mrs Lane, took her over to Lambeth where we were lately, and there did what I would with her but only the main thing, which she would not consent to, for which God be praised; and yet I came so near, that I was provoked to spend. But trust in the Lord I shall never do so again while I live ...

Samuel Pepys *Diary*

I was nearly a man now; I would be afraid of things no more; I would get out my pendulum, and see whether that would not help me. Not this time would I flinch from what consequences might follow. Let them be what they might, the pendulum should wag, and have a fair chance of doing its best.

I went up to my room, a sense of high emprise filling my little heart. Composedly, yea solemnly, I set to work, even as some enchanter of old might have drawn his circle, and chosen his spell out of his iron-clasped volume. I strode to the closet in which the awful instrument dwelt. It stood in the furthest corner. As I lifted it, something like a groan invaded my ear. My notions of locality were not then sufficiently developed to let me know

16

that grannie's room was on the other side of that closet. I almost let the creature, for as such I regarded it, drop. I was not to be deterred, however. I bore it carefully to the light, and set it gently on the window sill, full in view of the distant trees towards the west. I left it then for a moment, as if that it might gather its strength for its unwonted labours, while I closed the door, and, with what fancy I can scarcely imagine now, the curtains of my bed as well. Possibly it was with some notion of having one place to which, if the worst came to the worst, I might retreat for safety. Again I approached the window, and after standing for some time in contemplation of the pendulum, I set it in motion, and stood watching it.

It swung slower and slower. It wanted to stop. It should not stop. I gave it another swing. On it went, at first somewhat distractedly, next more regularly, then with slowly retarding movement. But it should not stop.

George MacDonald from *Wilfred Cumbermede*

❧

And in the midst of all, a fountaine stood,
Of richest substaunce, that on earth might bee,
So pure and shiny, that the siluer flood
Through euery channell running one might see;
Most goodly it with curious imageree
Was ouer-wrought, and shapes of naked boyes,
Of which some seemd with liuely iollitee,
To fly about, playing their wanton toyes,
Whilest others did them selues embay in liquid ioyes.

Edmund Spenser from *The Faerie Queene* (2.12)

17

We start, tremble, turn pale, and blush, as we are variously mov'd by imagination; and being a-bed, feel our bodies agitated with its power to that degree, as even sometimes to expire. And boyling youth when fast asleep, grows so warm with fancy, as in a dream to satisfie amorous desires.

> Ut quasi transactis sæpe omnibus rebus, profundant
> Fluminis ingentes fluctus vestemque cruentent.
> — *Lucret. l.* 4.

Who fansie gulling lyes, his enflam'd mind
Lays his love tribute there, where not design'd.

Montaigne *Essays*

Cleanly people often, when sound asleep, believing that they
are lifting their dress beside a urinal or the public vessels, pour
forth the filtered liquid of their whole body, and the Babylonian
coverlets of surpassing brilliancy are drenched. Then too those,
into the boiling currents of whose age seed is for the first time
passing, when the ripe fulness of days has produced it in their
limbs, idols encounter from without from what body soever,
harbingers of a glorious face and a beauteous bloom, which stir
and excite the appropriate portions of the frame and often
occasion fruitless anticipations of the pleasures of love.

Lucretius from *De Rerum Natura*
translated by H. A. J. Munro

The relation of Averroes, and now common in every mouth, of
the woman that conceived in a bath, by attracting the sperm or
seminal effluxion of a man admitted to bathe in some vicinity
unto her, I have scarce faith to believe; and had I been of the
Jury, should have hardly thought I had found the father in the
person that stood by her. 'Tis a new and unseconded way in
History to fornicate at a distance, and much offendeth the rules
of Physick, which say, there is no generation without a joynt
emission, nor only a virtual, but corporal and carnal contaction.

Generations by the Devil very improbable.

19

And although Aristotle and his adherents do cut off the one, who conceive no effectual ejaculation in women, yet in defence of the other they cannot be introduced. For, if as he believeth, the inordinate longitude of the organ, though in its proper recipient, may be a means to improlificate the seed; surely the distance of place, with the commixture of an aqueous body, must prove an effectual impediment, and utterly prevent the success of a conception. And therefore that conceit concerning the daughters of Lot, that they were impregnated by their sleeping father, or conceived by seminal pollution received at distance from him, will hardly be admitted. And therefore what is related of devils, and the contrived delusions of spirits, that they steal the seminal emissions of man, and transmit them into their votaries in coition, is much to be suspected; and altogether to be denied.

Sir Thomas Browne from Pseudodoxia Epidemica

⁂

31 July 1667 . . . I gather that the story I learned yesterday is true – that the King hath declared that he did not get the child of which she is conceived at this time, he having not as he says lain with her this half year; but she told him – 'God damn me! but you shall own it.' It seems he is jealous of Jermin and she loves him, so that the thoughts of his marrying of my Lady Falmouth puts her into fits of the mother. And he, it seems, hath lain with her from time to time continually, for a good while; and once, as this Cooling says, the King had like to have taken him a-bed with her, but that he was fain to creep under the bed into her closet. He says that for a good while the King's greatest pleasure hath been with his fingers, being able to do no more.

Samuel Pepys Diary

'I would do it a thousand times more,' said she, 'for the love of Christ.' In saying which she passed her hand across the flannel to the part above my knee, which I had equally complained of, and rubbed it also.

. . . .

The more she rubbed and the longer strokes she took, the more the fire kindled in my veins, till at length, by two or three strokes longer than the rest, my passion rose to the highest pitch. I seized her hand . . .

Laurence Sterne from Tristram Shandy

✺

The *Turks* have I know not how many black deformed Eunuchs (for the white serve for other ministeries) to this purpose sent commonly from *Egypt*, deprived in their childhood of all their privities, and brought up in the *Seraglio* at *Constantinople*, to keep their wives; which are so penned up they may not confer with any living man, or converse with younger women, have a Cucumber or Carrot sent in to them for their diet, but sliced, for fear, &c. and so live, and are left alone to their unchaste thoughts all the days of their lives.

Robert Burton from Anatomy of Melancholy

Sex in the Head

The boy who has been reading erotic poetry or looking at indecent pictures, if he then presses his body against a schoolfellow's, imagines himself only to be communing with him in an identical desire for a woman. How should he suppose that he is nòt like everybody else when he recognises the substance of what he feels on reading Mme. de Lafayette, Racine, Baudelaire, Walter Scott, at a time when he is still too little capable of observing himself to take into account what he has added from his own store to the picture, and that if the sentiment be the same the object differs, that what he desires is Rob Roy, and not Diana Vernon?

Marcel Proust from *Remembrance of Things Past*
translated by C. K. Scott-Moncrieff

≈

As you may guess, I was, like every other young girl, anxious to discover love and its pleasures. But since I had never been at a convent, nor made any close friendship, and since I lived under the eye of a vigilant mother, I had only the vaguest ideas on the subject, which I was quite unable to clarify. Nature herself, with whom since then I have certainly had every reason to be satisfied, had as yet given me no sign. One might almost have said that she was working in secret to the completion of her task. My mind alone was in a ferment: I had no wish to enjoy, I wanted to know, and the desire for knowledge suggested a means of acquiring it.

I realized that the only man I could speak to upon the subject without fear of compromise was my confessor. I made my decision immediately; overcoming a slight sense of shame, I laid claim to a sin I had not committed, accusing myself of having done 'everything that women do'. That was the expression I used, but in using it I had, in fact, no idea what it might convey. My hopes were not altogether disappointed, nor were they altogether fulfilled. My fear of betraying myself prevented my obtaining any explanation, but the good priest made so much of the crime that I concluded the pleasure of committing it must be extreme, and my desire for knowledge gave way to a desire for gratification.

Choderlos Laclos from *Les Liaisons Dangereuses*
translated by P. W. K. Stone

❧

13 *January* 1668 Stopped at Martins my bookseller, where I saw the French book which I did think to have had for my wife to translate, called *Escholle de Filles*; but when I came to look into it, it is the most bawdy, lewd book that ever I saw, rather worse than *putane errante* — so that I was ashamed of reading in it.
8 *February* 1668 Thence away to the Strand to my bookseller's, and there stayed an hour and bought that idle, roguish book *L'escholle des Filles*; which I have bought in plain binding (avoiding the buying of it better bound) because I resolve, as soon as I have read it, to burn it, so that it may not stand in the list of books nor among them, to disgrace them if it should be found.
9 *February* 1668. *Lords day*. We sang till almost night, and drank my good store of wine; and then they parted and I to my chamber, where I did read through *L'escholle des Filles*; a lewd book, but what doth me no wrong to read for information sake (but it did hazer my prick para stand all the while, and una vez to decharger); and after I had done it, I burned it, that it might not be among my books to my shame.

Samuel Pepys *Diary*

23

Sure he has got
Some bawdy pictures to call all this ging!
The friar and the nun; or the new motion
Of the knight's courser covering the parson's mare;
The boy of six year old with the great thing.

Ben Jonson from *The Alchemist*

✦

A liberal education had of course left him free to read the indecent passages in the school classics, but beyond a general sense of secrecy and obscenity in connection with his internal structure, had left his imagination quite unbiassed, so that for anything he knew his brain lay in small bags at his temples, and he had no more thought of representing to himself how his blood circulated than how paper served instead of gold. But the moment of vocation had come, and before he got down from his chair, the world was made new to him by a presentiment of endless processes filling the vast spaces planked out of his sight by that wordy ignorance which he had supposed to be knowledge. From that hour Lydgate felt the growth of an intellectual passion.

George Eliot from *Middlemarch*

✦

Antonia's mother, Elvira, considers the dangers of reading the Bible.

That prudent mother, while she admired the beauties of the sacred writings, was convinced that, unrestricted, no reading more improper could be permitted a young woman. Many of the

24

narratives can only tend to excite ideas the worst calculated for a female breast: everything is called plainly and roundly by its name, and the annals of a brothel would scarcely furnish a greater choice of indecent expressions. Yet this is the book which young women are recommended to study, which is put into the hands of children, able to comprehend little more than those passages of which they had better remain ignorant, and which but too frequently incalculates the first alarm to the still-sleeping passions. Of this was Elvira so fully convinced, that she would have preferred putting into her daughter's hands *Amadis de Gaul*, or *The Valiant Champion, Tirante the White*, and would sooner have authorized her studying the lewd exploits of *Don Galaor*, or the lascivious jokes of the *Damsel Plazer di mi vida*. She had in consequence made two resolutions respecting the Bible. The first was, that Antonia should not read it till she was of an age to feel its beauties and profit by its morality. The second, that it should be copied out with her own hand, and all improper passages either altered or omitted. She had adhered to this determination, and such was the Bible which Antonia was reading; it had been lately delivered to her, and she perused it with an avidity, with a delight that was inexpressible.

M. G. Lewis from *The Monk*

∼

Ermyntrude does some speculating in a letter to her friend, Esmeralda.

I've tried to go on with our enquiries about love and babies, but I haven't got much further. The other day I began edging round the conversation in that direction with old Simpson, and naturally that didn't succeed. She shut me up when I was still miles off. Everyone always does — that is, everyone who knows.

What can it mean. It is very odd. Why on earth should there be a secret about what happens when people have babies? I suppose it must be something appallingly shocking, but then, if it is, how can so many people bear to have them? Of course I'm quite sure it's got something to do with those absurd little things that men have in statues hanging between their legs, and that we haven't. And I'm also sure that it's got something to do with the thing between our legs that I always call my Pussy. I believe that may be it's real name, because once when I was at Oxford looking at the races with my cousin Tom, I heard quite a common woman say to another 'There, Sarah, doesn't that make your pussy pout?' And then I saw that one of the rowing men's trousers were all split and those things were showing between his legs; and it looked most extraordinary. I couldn't quite see enough, but the more I looked the more I felt — well, the more I felt my pussy pouting, as the woman had said. So now I call our's pussies and their's bow-wows, and my theory is that people have children when their bow-wows and pussies pout at the same time. Do you think that's it? Of course I can't imagine how it can possibly work, and I daresay I'm altogether wrong and it's really got something to do with W.C's.

Lord Folliot is coming to dinner, so I must go and dress. I'm sure he's a much worse bore than General Marchmont. He always will chuck me under the chin as though I was twelve. I hope you'll write again and tell me what you think about the pussies, the bow-wows, and the Mapletons. I promise you I won't show your letter to any one — even to Simpson — or Henry.

Your loving
Ermyntrude

P.S. What do you think castration means?

Lytton Strachey from *Ermyntrude and Esmeralda*

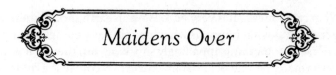

Maidens Over

Into love's spring-garden walk —
Virgins dangle on their stalk
Full-blown and playing at fifteen:
Come, bring your amorous sickles, then!
  See, they are pointing to their beds
  And call to reap their maidenheads.

James Shirley from *The Imposture*

❦

Roger caught himself wondering whether, at the worst, a little precursory love-making would do any harm. The ground might be gently tickled to receive his own sowing; the petals of the young girl's nature, playfully forced apart, would leave the golden heart of the flower but the more accessible to his own vertical rays.

Henry James from *Watch and Ward*

❦

Give me a wench about thirteen,
Already voted to the queen
Of lust and lovers; whose soft hair
Fann'd with the breath of gentle air,

O'er-spreads her shoulders like a tent,
And is her veil and ornament;
Whose tender touch will make the blood
Wild in the aged and the good;
Whose kisses, fasten'd to the mouth
Of three-score years and longer slouth,
Renew the age; and whose bright eye
Obscures those lesser lights of sky;
Whose snowy breasts (if we may call
That snow, that never melts at all,)
Makes Jove invent a new disguise,
In spite of Juno's jealousies;
Whose every part doth re-invite
The old decayed appetite;
And in whose sweet embraces I
May melt my self to lust, and die.
This is true bliss, and I confess
There is no other happiness.

Thomas Carew from 'The Second Rapture'

The dwarf, Quilp, plays with Little Nell.

'Has she come to sit upon Quilp's knee,' said the dwarf, in what he meant to be a soothing tone, 'or is she going to bed in her own little room inside here? Which is poor Nelly going to do?'

'What a remarkably pleasant way he has with children!' muttered Brass, as if in confidence between himself and the ceiling; 'upon my word it's quite a treat to hear him.'

'I'm not going to stay at all,' faltered Nell. 'I want a few things out of that room, and then I — I — won't come down here any more.'

'And a very nice little room it is!' said the dwarf, looking into it as the child entered. 'Quite a bower! You're sure you're not going to use it; you're sure you're not coming back, Nelly?'

'No,' replied the child, hurrying away, with the few articles of dress she had come to remove; 'never again! Never again.'

'She's very sensitive,' said Quilp, looking after her. 'Very sensitive; that's a pity. The bedstead is much about my size. I think I shall make it my little room.'

Charles Dickens from *The Old Curiosity Shop*

'Antonia, my charming Antonia!' exclaimed the monk, and caught her to his bosom; 'can I believe my senses? Repeat it to me, my sweet girl! Tell me again that you love me, that you love me truly and tenderly!'

'Indeed I do; let my mother be excepted, and the world holds no one more dear to me.'

At this frank avowal, Ambrosio no longer possessed himself; wild with desire, he clasped the blushing trembler in his arms. He fastened his lips greedily upon her's, sucked in her pure delicious breath, violated with his bold hand the treasures of her bosom, and wound around him her soft and yielding limbs. Startled, alarmed, and confused at his action, surprise at first deprived her of the power of resistance. At length recovering herself, she strove to escape from his embrace.

'Father! — Ambrosio!' she cried, 'release me, for God's sake!'

But the licentious monk heeded not her prayers: he persisted in his design, and proceeded to take still greater liberties. Antonia prayed, wept, and struggled: terrified to the extreme, though at what she knew not, she exerted all her strength to repulse the friar, and was on the point of shrieking for assistance, when the chamber door was suddenly thrown open. Ambrosio had just sufficient presence of mind to be sensible of his danger.

Reluctantly he quitted his prey, and started hastily from the couch. Antonia uttered an exclamation of joy, flew towards the door, and found herself clasped in the arms of her mother.

M. G. Lewis from *The Monk*

❦

BELINDA

. . . sure it must feel very strange to go to bed to a man!

LADY BRUTE

Um — it does feel a little odd at first, but it will soon grow easy to you.

Sir John Vanbrugh *The Provok'd Wife*

❦

Daphnis and Chloe, following the example of the animals in spring, begin to frolic.

. . . Here and there, not without pleasure, the blating of the flocks was heard, and the Lambs came skipping and inclined themselves obliquely under the damms to riggle and nussle at their dugs. But those which had not yet teemed, the Rams pursued; and when with some pains they had made them stand, one rid another. There were seen too the Chases of the he-goats, and their lascivious ardent leaps. Sometimes they had battels for the she's, and every one had his own wives, and kept them sollicitously, that no skulking adulterer should set upon them.

The old men seeing such incendiary fights as these, were prickt to Venus: but the Young, and such as of themselves did itch, and for some time had longed for the pleasure of Love, were wholly inflamed with what they heard, and melted away with what they saw, and lookt for something far more excelent then kisses and embraces were: and amongst them was Daphnis chief. Therefore he, as being now grown up and lusty by keeping at home, and following easie businesse all the Winter, was carried furiously to kissing, and stung with the desire to embrace, and close; and, in what he did, was now more curious, and more rampant then ever before. And therefore he began to ask of Chloe that she would give him free leave to do with her what he listed, and that she would lye naked with him naked, and longer too then they were wont: For there was nothing but that remaining of the Institutes of old Philetas, and that he would try, as the onely Canon, the onely med'cine to ease the pain of Love.

But Chloe asking him, whether anything remain'd more than kissing, embracing, and lying together upon the ground; or what he could do by lying naked upon a naked Girle?

That (quoth he) which the Rams use to do with the Ewes, and the he-Goats with the She's. Do you not see, how after that work, neither these run away, nor those weary themselves in pursuit of them; but afterwards how enjoying a common pleasure, they feed together quietly. That . . . as it seems is a sweet practice, and such as can master the bitternesse of Love.

How Daphnis? And dost thou not see the she-Goats and the Ewes, the he-Goats and the Rams, how these do their work standing, and those suffer standing too; these leaping and those admitting them upon their backs? And yet thou askest me to lye down, and that naked. But how much rougher are they then I, although I have all my Clothes on?

Daphnis is persuaded, and laying her down, lay down with her, and lay long; but knowing how to do nothing of that he was mad to do, lifted her up, and endeavour'd to imitate the Goats. But at the first finding a mere frustration there, he sate up, and lamented to himself, that he was more unskilfull than a very Tup in the practice of the mystery and the Art of Love . . .

Longus from *Daphnis and Chloe*

One day Cunégonde, while walking near the castle in a little wood which they called a park, saw Dr Pangloss in the bushes, giving a lesson in experimental physics to her mother's chamber-maid, a little brown wench, very pretty and very docile. As Miss Cunégonde had a great disposition for the sciences, she breathlessly observed the repeated experiments of which she was a witness; she clearly perceived the force of the doctor's reasons, the effects, and the causes; she turned back greatly flurried, quite pensive, and filled with the desire to be learned; dreaming that she might well be a sufficient reason for young Candide, and he for her.

She met Candide on reaching the castle and blushed; Candide blushed also; she wished him good morrow in a faltering tone, and Candide spoke to her without knowing what he said. The next day after dinner, as they went from table, Cunégonde and Candide found themselves behind a screen; Cunégonde let fall her handkerchief, Candide picked it up, she took him innocently by the hand, the youth as innocently kissed the young lady's hand with particular vivacity, sensibility, and grace; their lips met, their eyes sparkled, their knees trembled, their hands strayed. Baron Thunder-ten-Tronckh passed near the screen and beholding this cause and effect chased Candide from the castle with great kicks on the backside.

Voltaire from *Candide*
translated by John Butt

❧

Young Coridon and Phillis
    Sat in a lovely grove
Contriving crowns of lilies,
    Repeating tales of love:
And something else, but what I dare not name.

*   *   *   *   *

MAIDENS OVER

A thousand times he kissed her,
   Laying her on the green,
But as he further pressed her,
   Her pretty leg was seen:
And something else, but what I dare not name.

So many beauties removing
   His ardour still increased,
And greater joys pursuing
   He wandered o'er her breast:
And something else, but what I dare not name.

A last effort she trying
   His passion to withstand,
Cried (but it was faintly crying)
   'Pray take away your hand,
And something else, but what I dare not name.'

       *   *   *   *   *

The nymph seemed almost dying,
   Dissolved in amorous heat;
She kissed and told him sighing
   'My dear, your love is great:
And something else, but what I dare not name.'

Sir Charles Sedley from 'Young Coridon and Phillis'

Once he took her up to town to a *matinée* at one of the theatres, and was in anguish for a week afterwards, lest he had quickened some inherited tendency to dissipation. He used to lie awake at night, trying hard to fix in his mind the happy medium between coldness and weak fondness. With a heart full of tenderness, he used to measure out his caresses. He was in doubt for a long time as to what he should make her call him. At the outset he decided instinctively against 'papa'. It was a question between 'Mr Lawrence' and his baptismal name. He weighed the proprieties for a week, and then he determined the child should choose for herself. She had as yet avoided addressing him by name; at last he asked what name she preferred. She stared rather blankly at the time, but a few days afterwards he heard her shouting 'Roger!' from the garden under his window.

Henry James from *Watch and Ward*

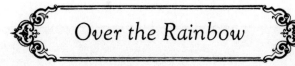
Over the Rainbow

14 O my dove, that art in the clefts of the rock, in the secret places of the stairs, let me see thy countenance, let me hear thy voice; for sweet is thy voice, and thy countenance is comely.
15 Take us the foxes, the little foxes, that spoil the vines: for our vines have tender grapes.
16 My beloved is mine, and I am his: he feedeth among the lilies.
17 Until the day break, and the shadows flee away, turn, my beloved, and be thou like a roe or a young hart upon the mountains of Bether.

Song of Solomon 2

The priest got up to take the crucifix; she craned her neck like someone who is thirsty and, pressing her lips to the body of God in the image of Man, she placed there with her last strength the most loving kiss she had ever given. Then he recited the Misereatur and the Indulgentiam, dipped his right thumb into the oil and began to anoint her: first her eyes, which had so coveted all earthly magnificence, then her nostrils, fond of gentle breezes and the scents of love; then her mouth which had opened to lie, which had groaned with pride and called out in sensual pleasure, then her hands, which delighted in sweet

contacts, and finally the soles of her feet, which had once run so fast towards the gratification of her desires.

Gustave Flaubert from *Madame Bovary*

❧

Now slides the silent meteor on, and leaves
A shining furrow, as thy thoughts in me.
Now folds the lily all her sweetness up,
And slips into the bosom of the lake.
So fold thyself, my dearest, thou, and slip
Into my bosom and be lost in me.

Alfred Lord Tennyson from *The Princess*

❧

These other impetuosities are very different. It is not we who apply the fuel; the fire is already kindled, and we are thrown into it in a moment to be consumed. It is by no efforts of the soul that it sorrows over the wound which the absence of our Lord has inflicted on it; it is far otherwise; for an arrow is driven into the entrails to the very quick, and into the heart at times, so that the soul knows not what is the matter with it, nor what it wishes for. It understands clearly enough that it wishes for God, and that the arrow seems tempered with some herb which makes the soul hate itself for the love of our Lord, and willingly lose its life for Him. It is impossible to describe or explain the way in which God wounds the soul, nor the very grievous pain inflicted, which deprives it of all self-consciousness; yet this pain is so sweet, that there is no joy in the world which gives greater delight. As I have just said, the soul would wish to be always dying of this wound.

St Teresa from *The Life of St Teresa*
translated by David Lewis

. . . which of our two large explosive hearts
So shook me? That, I know not. There were words
That broke in utterance . . . melted, in the fire, —
Embrace, that was convulsion, . . . then a kiss
As long and silent as the ecstatic night,
And deep, deep, shuddering breaths, which meant beyond
Whatever could be told by word or kiss.

Elizabeth Barrett Browning from *Aurora Leigh*

And as her silver body downward went,
With both her hands she made the bed a tent,
And in her own mind thought herself secure,
O'ercast with dim and darksome coverture.
And now she lets him whisper in her ear,
Flatter, entreat, promise, protest and swear,
Yet ever as he greedily assayed
To touch those dainties, she the harpy played,
And every limb did as a soldier stout
Defend the fort, and keep the foeman out.
For though the rising ivory mount he scaled,
Which is with azure circling lines empaled,
Much like a globe (a globe may I term this,
By which love sails to regions full of bliss),
Yet there with Sisyphus he toiled in vain,
Till gentle parley did the truce obtain.
Wherein Leander on her quivering breast
Breathless spoke something, and sighed out the rest.

Christopher Marlowe from *Hero and Leander*

2 I sleep, but my heart waketh: it is the voice of my beloved that knocketh, saying, Open to me, my sister, my love, my dove, my undefiled: for my head is filled with dew, and my locks with the drops of the night.

3 I have put off my coat; how shall I put it on? I have washed my feet; how shall I defile them?

4 My beloved put in his hand by the hole of the door, and my bowels were moved for him.

5 I rose up to open to my beloved; and my hands dropped with myrrh, and my fingers with sweet smelling myrrh, upon the handles of the lock.

6 I opened to my beloved; but my beloved had withdrawn himself, and was gone: my soul failed when he spake: I sought him, but I could not find him; I called him, but he gave me no answer.

Song of Solomon 5

On the Job

It is true that there is intense pleasure in sexual intercourse. The cause of this however is not that the semen is drawn from the whole body, but that there is violent stimulation; and that of course is why those who indulge often in such intercourse derive less pleasure from it. Moreover, the pleasure in fact comes at the end, but according to the theory it should occur (*a*) in every one of the parts, and (*b*) not simultaneously, but earlier in some and later in others.

Aristotle from *Generation of Animals*
translated by A. L. Peck

From the mysterious holy touch, such charms
Will flow as shall unlock her wreathèd arms,
And open a free passage to that fruit,
Which thou hast toiled for with a long pursuit.

     *   *   *   *   *

So shalt thou relish all, enjoy the whole
Delights of her fair body and pure soul:
Then boldly to the fight of love proceed;
'Tis mercy not to pity, though she bleed.
We'll strew no nuts, but change that ancient form,
For till to-morrow we'll prorogue this storm,
Which shall confound with its loud whistling noise
Her pleasing shrieks, and fan thy panting joys.

Thomas Carew from 'On the Marriage of T.K. and C.C.'

Nor when the youthful pair more closely join,
When hands in hands they lock, and thighs in thighs they twine,
Just in the raging foam of full desire
When both press on, both murmur, both expire,
They gripe, they squeeze, their humid tongues they dart,
As each would force their way to t'other's heart —
In vain: they only cruise about the coast,
For bodies cannot pierce, nor be in bodies lost,
As sure they strive to be when both engage
In that tumultuous momentary rage.
So tangled in the nets of love they lie,
Till man dissolves in that excess of joy.
Then when the gathered bag has burst its way
And ebbing tides the slackened nerves betray,
A pause ensues, and Nature nods a while,
Till with recruited rage new spirits boil;
And then the same vain violence returns,
With flames renewed th'erected furnace burns.

from Dryden's verse translation
of Lucretius' De Rerum Natura

*Venus' hair has been arranged for the evening by her
maidservant, Cosmé. It becomes disarranged.*

Cosmé's precise curls and artful waves had been finally disarranged at supper, and strayed ringlets of the black hair fell
loosely over Venus' soft, delicious, tired, swollen eyelids. Her
frail chemise and dear little drawers were torn and moist, and
clung transparently about her, and all her body was nervous and
responsive. Her closed thighs seemed like a vast replica of the
little bijou she had between them; the beautiful tétons du

43

derrière were firm as a plump virgin's cheek, and promised a joy as profound as the mystery of the Rue Vendôme, and the minor chevelure, just profuse enough, curled as prettily as the hair upon a cherub's head.

Tannhauser, pale and speechless with excitement, passed his gem-girt fingers brutally over the divine limbs, tearing away smock and pantalon and stocking, and then, stripping himself of his own few things, fell upon the splendid lady with a deep-drawn breath!

Aubrey Beardsley from Under the Hill

❧

Doing, a filthy pleasure is, and short;
And done, we straight repent us of the sport:
Let us not then rush blindly on unto it,
Like lustful beasts, that only know to do it:
For lust will languish, and that heat decay,
But thus, thus, keeping endless Holy-day,
Let us together closely lie, and kiss,
There is no labour, nor no shame in this;
This hath pleased, doth please and long will please; never
Can this decay, but is beginning ever.

Petronius translated from the Latin by Ben Jonson

❧

12 January 1763 . . . I came softly into the room, and in a sweet delirium slipped into bed and was immediately clasped in her snowy arms and pressed to her milk-white bosom. Good heavens, what a loose did we give to amorous dalliance! The friendly curtain of darkness concealed our blushes. In a moment

44

I felt myself animated with the strongest power of love, and, from my dearest creature's kindness, had a most luscious feast. Proud of my godlike vigour, I soon resumed the noble game. I was in full glow of health. Sobriety had preserved me from effeminacy and weakness, and my bounding blood beat quick and high alarms. A more voluptuous night I never enjoyed. Five times was I fairly lost in supreme rapture. Louisa was madly fond of me; she declared I was a prodigy, and asked me if this was not extraordinary for human nature. I said twice as much might be, but this was not, although in my own mind I was somewhat proud of my performance. She said it was what there was no just reason to be proud of. But I told her I could not help it. She said it was what we had in common with the beasts. I said no. For we had it highly improved by the pleasures of sentiment. I asked her what she thought enough. She gently chid me for asking such questions, but said two times.

James Boswell *Journals*

In the vigour of his age he [Gargantua's father] married Gargamelle, daughter to the king of the Parpaillons, a jolly pug, and well-mouthed wench. These two did oftentimes do the two-backed beast together, joyfully rubbing and frotting their bacon against one another, in so far, that at last she became great with child of a fair son, and went with him unto the eleventh month.

Rabelais from *Gargantua and Pantagruel*
translated by Sir Thomas Urquhart

45

These lovers cry — Oh! oh! they die!
    Yet that which seems the wound to kill
Doth turn oh! oh! to ha! ha! he!
    So dying love lives still:
Oh! oh! a while, but ha! ha! ha!
Oh! oh! groans out for ha! ha! ha!
Heigh-ho!

William Shakespeare from *Troilus and Cressida*

❧

For, as we erst have sung, the seeds of life
First spring when manhood first the frame confirms.
And as on various functions various powers
Alone can act propulsive, human seeds
By nought but human beauty can be rous'd.
These, when once gender'd from their cells minute
O'er every limb, o'er every organ spread,
Crowd in full concourse tow'rds the nervous fount

By nature rear'd appropriate; whence abrupt
Excite they oft, as forms of beauty rise,
The scenes at hand, the regions ruled by love.
Then springs the tender tumor, the warm wish
Full o'er the foe, the luscious wound who deals,
With dext'rous aim to pour the high-wrought charge,
And full contending in the genial fight.
So falls the victim on the part assail'd;
With the red blood the glist'ning bruise so swells;
And o'er th' assassin flows the tide he draws.

from Dryden's verse translation
of Lucretius' *De Rerum Natura*

❧

Then I clasped her in my arms. And again my whole body
responded to the rich inexhaustible presence of her own. Yet
again I gauged the potency to comfort, the sudden exultation,
the overwhelming intoxication that welled out from her breasts
and belly, merely by their soft pressure against me; and my
hands caressed the gorgeous resilient wedges of her back and
waist, and my lips fastened themselves to a mysterious point I
had picked out in her curving neck. My natural impulse would
have been to break off these delightful joys of the meal to lead
Lucienne to the bed. It seemed to me as if only the deep
interactions of the act of possession could shake off the evil
influence which the visit to the ship had cast over us, and only
the extreme limits of sensual delight blind us to the true relation
of the present to the future. And that in that way we could
believe, with some slight good will, that the intensity and
perfection of the moment had by some magical operation
succeeded in modifying the rhythm of time and the inevitability
of events.

Jules Romains from *The Body's Rapture*
translated by John Rodker

In vegetal creatures what sovereignty Love hath by many pregnant proofs and familiar examples may be proved, especially of palm trees, which are both he and she, and express not a sympathy but a love-passion, as by many observations have been confirmed.

> Vivunt in venerem frondes, omnisque vicissim
> Felix arbor amat, nutant ad mutua palmæ
> Fœdera, populeo suspirat populus ictu,
> Et platani platanis, alnoque assibilat alnus.*

Constantine gives an instance out of *Florentius* his Georgicks, of a Palm-tree that loved most fervently, *and would not be comforted until such time her Love applied himself unto her; you might see the two trees bend, and of their own accords stretch out their bows to embrace and kiss each other: they will give manifest signs of mutual love.*

*Boughs live for love, and every flourishing tree in turn feels the passion: palms nod mutual vows, poplar sighs to poplar, plane to plane, and alder murmurs to alder.

Robert Burton from *The Anatomy of Melancholy*

❧

I was a child beneath her touch, — a man
  When breast to breast we clung, even I and she, —
  A spirit when her spirit looked through me, —
A god when all our life-breath met to fan
Our life-blood, till love's emulous ardours ran,
  Fire within fire, desire in deity.

Dante Gabriel Rossetti from 'The Kiss'

3 June 1666 I to St Margaret's Westminster, and there saw at church my pretty Betty Michell. And thence to the Abbey, and so to Mrs Martin and there did what je voudrais avec her, both devante and backward, which is also muy bon plazer.

Samuel Pepys *Diary*

❧

And here and there I had her,
And everywhere I had her,
Her toy was such, that every touch
Would make a lover madder.

Sir George Etherege from *She would if she could*

❧

He erected a noble altar monument of marble whereon his effigies in armour lay; at the feet was the *Effigies* of his mistresse, Mris Anne Vavasour. Which occasioned these verses:

Here lies the good old Knight Sir Harry,
Who loved well, but would not marry;
While he lived, and had his feeling,
She did lye, and he was kneeling,
Now he's dead and cannot feele
He doeth lye and shee doeth kneele.

Some Bishop did threaten to have this Monument defaced; at least, to remove Mris A. Vavasour's *effigies*.

'Sir Henry Lee' from *Aubrey's Brief Lives*
edited by Oliver Lawson Dick

49

ON THE JOB

Soon shalt thou hear the Bridegroom's voice,
The midnight cry, 'Behold, I come!'

from a hymn by H. Bonar in *Public School Hymn Book*

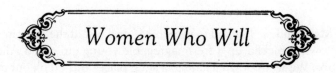

Women Who Will

Nor does the woman sigh always with fictitious love, when she locks in her embrace and joins with her body the man's body and holds it, sucking his lips into her lips and drinking in his kisses. Often she does it from the heart, and seeking mutual joys courts him to run the complete race of love. And in no other way could birds cattle wild-beasts sheep and mares submit to bear the males, except because the very exuberance of nature in the females is in heat and burns and joyously draws in the Venus of the covering males.

Lucretius from *De Rerum Natura*
translated by H. A. J. Munro

✿

There cam a soger here to stay,
    He swore he wadna steer me;
But, lang before the break o' day,
    He cuddl'd muddl'd near me:
He set a stiff thing to my wame,
    I docht na bide the bends o't;
But lang before the grey morn cam,
    I soupl'd baith the ends o't.

Robert Burns song from
The Merry Muses of Caledonia

51

17 May 1763 . . . I sallied to the streets, and just at the bottom of our own, I picked up a fresh, agreeable young girl called Alice Gibbs. We went down a lane to a snug place, and I took out my armour, but she begged that I might not put it on, as the sport was much pleasanter without it, and as she was quite safe. I was so rash as to trust her, and had a very agreeable congress.

James Boswell *Journals*

❧

Her arms the joyful conqueror embrace,
And seem to guide me to the sought-for place:
Her love is in her sparkling eyes express'd
She falls o' the bed for pleasure more than rest.

Sir George Etherege from 'The Imperfect Enjoyment'

❧

Mris Elizabeth Broughton was daughter of Edward Broughton of Herefordshire, an ancient Family. Her father lived at the Mannour-house at Cannon-Peon. Whether he was borne there or no, I know not; but there she lost her Mayden-head to a poor young fellow, then I beleeve handsome, but, in 1660, a pittifull poor old weaver, Clarke of the Parish. He had fine curled haire, but gray. Her father at length discovered her inclinations and locked her up in the Turret of the house, but she getts down by a rope; and away she gott to London, and did sett up for her selfe.

She was a most exquisite beautie, as finely shaped as Nature could frame; had a delicate Witt. She was soon taken notice of at London, and her price was very deare — a second Thais. Richard,

Earle of Dorset, kept her (whether before or after Venetia I know
not, but I guess before). At last she grew common and infamous
and gott the Pox, of which she died.

'Elizabeth Broughton' from *Aubrey's Brief Lives*
edited by Oliver Lawson Dick

✣

*Having dropped into a tailor's shop to ask the way to the
Opéra, the narrator is prompted by the beauty of the serving
girl to ask for a pair of gloves.*

The beautiful Griffet rofe up when I faid this, and going behind
the counter, reached down a parcel and untied it: I advanced to
the fide over againft her: they were all too large. The beautiful
Griffet meafured them one by one acrofs my hand — It would
not alter the dimenfions — She begged I would try a fingle pair,
which feemed to be the leaft — She held it open — my hand
flipped into it at once — It will not do, faid I, fhaking my head a
little — No, faid fhe, doing the fame thing.

There are certain combined looks of fimple fubtlety — where
whim, and fenfe, and ferioufnefs, and nonfenfe, are fo blended,
that all the language of Babel fet loofe together could not exprefs
them — they are communicated and caught fo inftantaneoufly,
that you can fcarce fay which party is the infecter. I leave it to
your men of words to fwell pages about it — it is enough in the
prefent to fay again, the gloves would not do; fo folding our
hands within our arms, we both loll'd upon the counter — it was
narrow, and there was juft room for the parcel to ly between us.

The beautiful Griffet looked fometimes at the gloves, then
fideways to the window, then at the gloves — and then at me. I
was not difpofed to break filence — I followed her example: fo I
looked at the gloves, then to the window, then at the gloves, and
then at her — and fo on alternately.

I found I loft confiderably in every attack — fhe had a quick black eye, and fhot through two fuch long and filken eye-lafhes with fuch penetration, that fhe looked into my very heart and reins — It may feem ftrange, but I could actually feel fhe did — It is no matter, faid I, taking up a couple of the pairs next me, and putting them into my pocket.

Laurence Sterne from A *Sentimental Journey*

᠅

4 Say unto wisdom, Thou art my sister; and call understanding thy kinswoman:
5 That they may keep thee from the strange woman, from the stranger which flattereth with her words.
6 For at the window of my house I looked through my casement,
7 And beheld among the simple ones, I discerned among the youths, a young man void of understanding,
8 Passing through the street near her corner; and he went the way to her house,
9 In the twilight, in the evening, in the black and dark night:
10 And, behold, there met him a woman with the attire of an harlot, and subtil of heart.
11 (She is loud and stubborn; her feet abide not in her house:
12 Now is she without, now in the streets, and lieth in wait at every corner.)
13 So she caught him, and kissed him, and with an impudent face said unto him,
14 I have peace offerings with me; this day have I payed my vows.
15 Therefore came I forth to meet thee, diligently to seek thy face, and I have found thee.
16 I have decked my bed with coverings of tapestry, with carved works, with fine linen of Egypt.
17 I have perfumed my bed with myrrh, aloes, and cinnamon.
18 Come, let us take our fill of love until the morning: let us solace ourselves with loves.
19 For the goodman is not at home, he is gone a long journey:
20 He hath taken a bag of money with him, and will come home at the day appointed.
21 With her much fair speech she caused him to yield, with the flattering of her lips she forced him.
22 He goeth after her straightway, as an ox goeth to the slaughter, or as a fool to the correction of the stocks;
23 Till a dart strike through his liver; as a bird hasteth to the snare, and knoweth not that it is for his life.

Proverbs 7

A trapper sees Enkidu, created by the goddess Aruru to equal Gilgamesh in strength, and reports to the giant.

The trapper set out on his journey to Uruk and addressed himself to Gilgamesh saying, 'A man unlike any other is roaming now in the pastures; he is as strong as a star from heaven and I am afraid to approach him. He helps the wild game to escape; he fills in my pits and pulls up my traps.' Gilgamesh said, 'Trapper, go back, take with you a harlot, a child of pleasure. At the drinking-hole he will embrace her and the game of the wilderness will surely reject him.'

Now the trapper returned, taking the harlot with him. After a three days' journey they came to the drinking-hole, and there they sat down; the harlot and the trapper sat facing one another and waited for the game to come. For the first day and for the second day the two sat waiting, but on the third day the herds came; they came down to drink and Enkidu was with them. The small wild creatures of the plains were glad of the water, and Enkidu with them, who ate grass with the gazelle and was born in the hills; and she saw him, the savage man, come from far-off in the hills. The trapper spoke to her: 'There he is. Now, woman, make your breasts bare, have no shame, do not delay but welcome his love. Let him see you naked, let him possess your body. When he comes near uncover yourself and lie with him; teach him, the savage man, your woman's art, for when his love is drawn to you the wild beasts that shared his life in the hills will reject him.'

She was not ashamed to take him, she made herself naked and welcomed his eagerness, she incited the savage to love and taught him the woman's art. For six days and seven nights they lay together, for Enkidu had forgotten his home in the hills; but when he was satisfied he went back to the wild beasts. Then, when the gazelle saw him, they bolted away; when the wild creatures saw him they fled. Enkidu would have followed, but his body was bound as though with a cord, his knees gave way when he started to run, his swiftness was gone. And now the

56

wild creatures had all fled away; Enkidu was grown weak, for wisdom was in him, and the thoughts of a man were in his heart.

from *The Epic of Gilgamesh*
translated by N. K. Sandars

༄

Whil'st Alexis lay prest
In her arms he lov'd best,
With his hands round her neck,
And his head on her breast,
He found the fierce pleasure too hasty to stay,
And his soul in the tempest just flying away.

When Cælia saw this,
With a sigh, and a kiss,
She cry'd, Oh my dear, I am robb'd of my bliss;
'Tis unkind to your Love, and unfaithfully done,
To leave me behind you, and die all alone.

The Youth, though in haste,
And breathing his last,
In pity dy'd slowly, while she dy'd more fast;
Till at length she cry'd, Now, my dear, now let us go,
Now die, my Alexis, and I will die too.

Thus intranc'd they did lie,
Till Alexis did try
To recover new breath, that again he might die:
Then often they di'd; but the more they did so,
The Nymph di'd more quick, and the Shepherd more slow.

John Dryden from *Marriage à la Mode*

No woman was happier in her choice — no woman — And after above two months of uninterrupted intercourse, there is still more and more cause for thankfulness; — and more and more affection on his side — He loves me better every day, he says . . . My health improves still, too.

Elizabeth Barrett Browning from a letter to a friend

⁓ℳↄ

Laura succumbs to the temptations of the Goblin Market and has to be rescued by her sister, Lizzie, who braves the goblins for her sake.

They answered all together:
'Buy from us with a golden curl.'
She clipped a precious golden lock,
She dropped a tear more rare than pearl,
Then sucked their fruit globes fair or red.
Sweeter than honey from the rock,
Stronger than man-rejoicing wine,
Clearer than water flowed that juice;
She never tasted such before,
How should it cloy with length of use?
She sucked and sucked and sucked the more
Fruits which that unknown orchard bore;
She sucked until her lips were sore;

       *   *   *   *   *

She cried, 'Laura,' up the garden,
'Did you miss me?
Come and kiss me.

Never mind my bruises,
Hug me, kiss me, suck my juices
Squeezed from goblin fruits for you,
Goblin pulp and goblin dew.
Eat me, drink me, love me;
Laura, make much of me;
For your sake I have braved the glen
And had to do with goblin merchant men.'

Christina Rossetti from 'Goblin Market'

❧

Though abandoned by her husband, Roxana has no difficulty in finding protectors.

About one o'clock in the morning, for so long we sat up together, I said, Come, 'tis one o'clock, I must go to bed. Well, says he, I'll go with you. No, no, says I, go to your own chamber. He said he would go to bed with me. Nay, says I, if you will, I don't know what to say; if I can't help it, you must. However, I got from him, left him, and went into my chamber, but did not shut the door, and, as he could easily see that I was undressing myself, he steps to his own room, which was but on the same floor, and in a few minutes undresses himself also, and returns to my door in his gown and slippers.

I thought he had been gone indeed, and so that he had been in jest; and, by the way, thought either he had no mind to the thing, or that he never intended it; so I shut my door, that is, latched it, for I seldom locked or bolted it, and went to bed. I had not been in bed a minute, but he comes in his gown to the door, and opens it a little way, but not enough to come in, or look in, and says softly, What, are you really gone to bed? Yes, yes, says I, get you gone. No, indeed, says he, I shall not be gone, you gave me leave before to come to bed, and you shan't say get you gone now. So he comes into my room, and then turns about, and fastens the door, and immediately comes to the bedside to me. I pretended to scold and struggle, and bid him begone, with more warmth than before; but it was all one; he had not a rag of clothes on but his gown and slippers and shirt, so he throws off his gown, and throws open the bed, and came in at once.

I made a seeming resistance, but it was no more indeed; for, as above, I resolved from the beginning he should lie with me if he would, and for the rest I left it to come after.

Well, he lay with me that night, and the two next, and very merry we were all the three days between . . .

Daniel Defoe from Roxana

❧

'Come rede me, dame, come tell me, dame,
   'My dame come tell me truly,
'What length o' graith, when weel ca'd hame,
   'Will sair a woman duly?'
The carlin clew her wanton tail,
   Her wanton tail sae ready —
I learn'd a sang in Annandale,
   Nine inch will please a lady. —

But for a koontrie c — —t like mine,
   In sooth, we're nae sae gentle;
We'll tak tway thumb-bread to the nine,
   And that's a sonsy p— —ntle:
O Leeze me on my Charlie lad,
   I'll ne'er forget my Charlie!
Tawy roarin handfu's and a daud,
   He nidge't it in fu' rarely. —

60

But weary fa' the laithron doup,
    And may it ne'er be thrivin!
It's no the length that maks me loup,
    But it's the double drivin. —
Come nidge me, Tam, come nudge me, Tam,
    Come nidge me o'er the nyvel!
Come lowse & lug your battering ram,
    And thrash him at my gyvel!

Robert Burns song from *The Merry Muses of Caledonia*

There, whence that Musick seemed heard to bee,
Was the faire Witch her selfe now solacing,
With a new Louer, whom through sorceree
And witchcraft, she from farre did thither bring:
There she had him now layd a slombering,
In secret shade, after long wanton ioyes:
Whilst round about them pleasauntly did sing
Many faire Ladies, and lasciuious boyes,
That euer mixt their song with light licentious toyes.

And all that while, right ouer him she hong,
With her false eyes fast fixed in his sight,
As seeking medicine, whence she was stong,
Or greedily depasturing delight:
And oft inclining downe with kisses light,
For feare of waking him, his lips bedewd,
And through his humid eyes did sucke his spright,
Quite molten into lust and pleasure lewd;
Wherewith she sighed soft, as if his case she rewd.

Edmund Spenser from *The Faerie Queene* (2.2.)

The word of the LORD came again unto me, saying,
2 Son of man, there were two women, the daughters of one mother:
3 And they committed whoredoms in Egypt; they committed whoredoms in their youth: there were their breasts pressed, and there they bruised the teats of their virginity.
4 And the names of them were Aholah the elder, and Aholibah her sister: and they were mine, and they bare sons and daughters. Thus were their names; Samaria is Aholah, and Jerusalem Aholibah.
5 And Aholah played the harlot when she was mine; and she doted on her lovers, on the Assyrians her neighbours,
6 Which were clothed with blue, captains and rulers, all of them

62

desirable young men, horsemen riding upon horses.

7 Thus she committed her whoredoms with them, with all them that were the chosen men of Assyria, and with all on whom she doted: with all their idols she defiled herself.

8 Neither left she her whoredoms brought from Egypt: for in her youth they lay with her, and they bruised the breasts of her virginity, and poured their whoredom upon her.

9 Wherefore I have delivered her into the hand of her lovers, into the hand of the Assyrians, upon whom she doted.

10 These discovered her nakedness: they took her sons and her daughters, and slew her with the sword: and she became famous among women; for they had executed judgment upon her.

11 And when her sister Aholibah saw this, she was more corrupt in her inordinate love than she, and in her whoredoms more than her sister in her whoredoms.

12 She doted upon the Assyrians her neighbours, captains and rulers clothed most gorgeously, horsemen riding upon horses, all of them desirable young men.

13 Then I saw that she was defiled, that they took both one way,

14 And that she increased her whoredoms: for when she saw men pourtrayed upon the wall, the images of the Chaldeans pourtrayed with vermilion,

15 Girded with girdles upon their loins, exceeding in dyed attire upon their heads, all of them princes to look to, after the manner of the Babylonians of Chaldea, the land of their nativity:

16 And as soon as she saw them with her eyes, she doted upon them, and sent messengers unto them into Chaldea.

17 And the Babylonians came to her into the bed of love, and they defiled her with their whoredom, and she was polluted with them, and her mind was alienated from them.

18 So she discovered her whoredoms, and discovered her nakedness: then my mind was alienated from her, like as my mind was alienated from her sister.

19 Yet she multiplied her whoredoms, in calling to remembrance the days of her youth, wherein she had played the harlot in the land of Egypt.

20 For she doted upon their paramours, whose flesh is as the flesh of asses, and whose issue is like the issue of horses.

21 Thus thou calledst to remembrance the lewdness of thy youth, in bruising thy teats by the Egyptians for the paps of thy youth.

Ezekiel 23

63

Even now, though it is five-and-twenty years ago, people remember Lady O'Dowd performing a jig at Government House, where she danced down two Aides-de-Camp, a Major of Madras Cavalry, and two gentlemen of the Civil Service; and, persuaded by Major Dobbin, C.B., second in command of the — th, to retire to the supper-room, *lassata nondum satiata recessit.*

William Thackeray from *Vanity Fair*

❧

Her venal charms were abandoned to a promiscuous crowd of citizens and strangers, of every rank, and of every profession; the fortunate lover who had been promised a night of enjoyment was often driven from her bed by a stronger or more wealthy favourite; and, when she passed through the streets, her presence was avoided by all who wished to escape either the scandal or the temptation ... After exhausting the arts of sensual pleasure,* she most ungratefully murmured against the parsimony of Nature; but her murmurs, her pleasures, and her arts must be veiled in the obscurity of a learned language.

*At a memorable supper, thirty slaves waited round the table; ten young men feasted with Theodora. Her charity was *universal.* Et lassata viris, necdum satiata, recessit (Tired out by men but not yet satisfied she withdrew).

Edward Gibbon from *The Decline and Fall of the Roman Empire*

❧

The author finds that his transformation into an ass is not
without its perks.

There fortuned to be amongst the assembly a noble and rich
matron, that after that she had paid her due to behold me was
greatly delighted with all my tricks and qualities, in so much that
she fell marvellously in love with me, and could find no remedy
to her passions and disordinate appetite, but continually desired
to have her pleasure with me, like a new Pasiphae, but with an
ass. In the end she promised a great reward to my keeper for the
custody of me one night, who cared for naught but for gain of a
little money, and accorded to her desire. When therefore I had
supped in a parlour with my master, we departed away and went
into our chamber, where we found the fair matron, who had
tarried a great space for our coming. Good God, how nobly all
things there were prepared! There were four eunuchs that laid a
bed of billowing down on the ground with bolsters accordingly
for us to lie on; the coverlet was of cloth of gold and Tyrian dye,
and the pillows small, but soft and tender, as whereon delicate
matrons accustom to lay their heads. Then the eunuchs, not
minding to delay any longer the pleasure of their mistress, closed
the doors of the chamber and departed away; and within the
chamber were wax candles that made light the darkness of the
night all the place over. Then she put off all her garments to her
naked skin, yea even the veil of her bosom, and standing next
the lamp began to anoint all her body with balm, and mine
likewise, but especially my nose; which done, she kissed me, not
as they accustom to do at the stews or in brothel-houses, or in the
courtesan schools for gain of money, but purely, sincerely, and
with great affection, casting out these and like loving words:
'Thou art he whom I love,' 'Thou art he whom I only desire,'
'Without thee I cannot live,' and other like preamble of talk, as
women can use well enough when they mind to shew or declare
their burning passions and great affection of love. Then she took
me by the halter and cast me upon the bed, which was nothing

strange unto me, considering that she was so beautiful a matron, and I so well blown out with wine, and perfumed with balm, whereby I was readily prepared for the purpose. But nothing grieved me so much as to think how I should with my huge and great legs embrace so fair a matron, or how I should touch her fine, dainty, and silken skin made of milk and honey with my hard hoofs, or how it was possible to kiss her soft, her pretty and ruddy lips with my monstrous great mouth and stony teeth, or how she, who was so young and tender, could receive my love. And I verily thought if I should hurt the woman by any kind of means, I should be thrown out to the wild beasts: but in the mean season she spoke gently to me, kissing me oft, and looked on me with burning eyes, saying: 'I hold thee my cony, I hold thee my nops, my sparrow,' and therewithal she shewed me that all my fear was vain, for she oft-times embraced my body round about, and had her pleasure with me, whereby I thought the mother of Minotaurus did not causeless quench her inordinate desire with a bull.

Apuleius from *The Golden Ass*
translated by W. Adlington

Hark! how in yonder shady grove
Sweet Philomel is warbling love
And with her voice is courting kings –
For since she was a bird she sings:
   There is no pleasure but in men,
   O come and ravish me again!

James Shirley from *The Imposture*

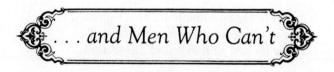

... and Men Who Can't

Come to the temple where I should adore
My Saint, I worship at the sacred door.
Oh, cruel chance! the town, which did oppose
My strength so long, now yields to my dispose;
When overjoy'd with victory I fall
Dead at the foot of the surrendered wall,
Without the usual ceremony, we
Have both fulfilled the amorous mystery;
The action which we should have jointly done,
Each has unluckily perform'd alone;
The union which our bodies should enjoy,
The union of our eager souls destroy.
Our flames are punished by their own excess,
We'd had more pleasure had our loves been less.
She blushed and frown'd perceiving we had done
The sport she thought we scarce had yet begun.

Sir George Etherege from 'The Imperfect Enjoyment'

❧

And now without respect or fear
He seeks the object of his vows;
His love no modesty allows:
By swift degrees advancing there,
His daring hand that altar seized
Where gods of love do sacrifice,
That awful throne, that paradise

Where rage is tamed and anger pleased,
That living fountain from whose trills
The melted soul in liquid drops distils.

*   *   *   *   *

He saw how at her length she lay,
He saw her rising bosom bare,
Her loose thin robes through which appear
A shape designed for love and play:
Abandoned by her pride and shame
She does her softest sweets dispense,
Offering her virgin innocence
A victim to love's sacred flame —
Whilst the o'er-ravished shepherd lies
Unable to perform the sacrifice.

*   *   *   *   *

Ready to taste a thousand joys
The too-transported hapless swain
Found the vast pleasure turned to pain —
Pleasure which too much love destroys!
The willing garment by he laid
And, heaven all open to his view,
Mad to possess, himself he threw
On the defenceless lovely maid;
But O what envious gods conspire
To snatch his power yet leave him the desire!

Aphra Behn from 'The Disappointment'

68

This dart of love, whose piercing point, oft tried
With virgin blood, ten thousand maids has dyed;
Which nature still directed with such art
That it through every cunt reached every heart;
Stiffly resolved, 'twould carelessly invade
Woman or boy, nor aught its fury stayed
Where'er it pierced — a cunt it found or made —
Now languid lies, in this unhappy hour,
Shrunk up, and sapless, like a withered flower.

Lord Rochester from 'The Imperfect Enjoyment'

69

Sour Puss

I wonder why the chaster of your sex
Should think this pretty toy called maidenhead
So strange a loss, when, being lost, 'tis nothing,
And you are still the same.

John Ford from *'Tis Pity She's a Whore*

Leontes, King of Sicily, suspects that his wife Hermione is carrying on with Poliximes, King of Bohemia.

– Go, play, boy, play. – There have been,
Or I am much deceiv'd, cuckolds ere now;
And many a man there is, even at this present,
Now while I speak this, holds his wife by th'arm,
That little thinks she has been sluic'd in's absence,
And his pond fish'd by his next neighbour, by
Sir Smile, his neighbour: nay, there's comfort in't,
Whiles other men have gates, and those gates open'd,
As mine, against their will: should all despair
That have revolted wives, the tenth of mankind
Would hang themselves. Physic for't there's none.
It is a bawdy planet, that will strike
Where 'tis predominant; and 'tis powerful, think it,
From east, west, north, and south: be it concluded,
No barricado for a belly; know't;

It will let in and out the enemy
With bag and baggage: many thousand on's
Have the disease, and feel't not.

William Shakespeare from *The Winter's Tale*

✿

For me,
I confess, William, and avow to thee,
(Soft in thine ear) that such sweet female whims
As nasty backsides out and wriggled limbs
Nor bitch-squeaks, nor the smell of heated quims
Are not a passion of mine naturally.

Dante Gabriel Rossetti from 'The Can-Can at Valentino's'

✿

*Ovid instructs his mistress on how to behave in the presence
of her husband at a feast to which he has been invited.*

Do not allow him to press your neck, by putting his arms around
it; nor recline your gentle head on his unsightly breast. Let not
your bosom, or your breasts so close at hand, admit his fingers;
and especially allow him to give you no kisses. If you do give him
any kisses, I shall be discovered to be your lover, and I shall say,
'Those are my own,' and shall be laying hands upon him.

Still, this I shall be able to see; but what the clothing carefully
conceals, the same will be a cause for me of apprehension full of
doubts. Touch not his thigh with yours, and cross not legs with
him, and do not unite your delicate foot with his uncouth leg. To

my misery, I am apprehensive of many a thing, because many a thing have I done in my wantonness; and I myself am tormented, through fear of my own precedent. Oft by joining hands beneath the cloth, have my mistress and I forestalled our hurried delights. This, I am sure, you will not do for him; but that you may not even be supposed to do so, take away the conscious covering from your bosom.

Ovid from the *Amores*

Mr Wiseman answers Mr Attentive's questions about the recently deceased Mr Badman.

Badmans Atten. *But did not Mr. Badman marry again quickly?*
ˀ   Wise. No, not a good while after: and when he was asked the
ʒuage. reason, he would make this slightly answer, *Who would keep a Cow of their own, that can have a quart of milk for a penny?* Meaning, Who would be at the charge to have a Wife, that can have a Whore when he listeth?

John Bunyan from *The Life and Death of Mr Badman*

Mirabell, engaged to Oriana, still has an aversion to marriage.

Why should I be at charge to keep a wife of mine own,
When other honest married men will ease me,
And thank me too, and be beholding to me?
Thou think'st I am mad for a maidenhead; thou art cozened:

Or if I were addicted to that diet,
Can you tell me where I should have one? thou art eighteen now,
And, if thou hast thy maidenhead yet extant,
Sure 'tis as big as cods-head; those grave dishes
I never love to deal withal. Dost thou see this book here?
Look over all these ranks: all these are women,
Maids and pretenders to maidenheads: these are my conquests

*　　*　　*　　*　　*

And I enjoyed 'em at my will and left 'em:
Some of 'em are married since and were as pure maids again.

John Fletcher from *The Wild-Goose Chase*

Master Carvel became as jealous as a tiger, and entered into a
very profound suspicion that his new-married gixy did keep a-
buttock-stirring with others. To prevent which inconveniency,
he did tell her many tragical stories of the total ruin of several
kingdoms by adultery; did read unto her the legend of chaste
wives; then made some lectures to her in the praise of the choice
virtue of pudicity, and did present her with a book in
commendation of conjugal fidelity, wherein the wickedness of
all licentious women was odiously detested; and withal he gave
her a chain enriched with pure oriental sapphires. Notwith-
standing all this, he found her always more and more inclined to
the reception of her neighbour copes-mates, that day by day his
jealousy increased. In sequel whereof, one night as he was lying
by her, whilst in his sleep the rambling fancies of the lecherous
deportments of his wife did take up the cellules of his brain, he
dreamt that he encountered with the devil, to whom he had
discovered to the full the buzzing of his head, and suspicion that
his wife did tread her shoe awry. The devil, he thought, in this

perplexity, did for his comfort give him a ring, and therewithal did kindly put it on his middle finger, saying, Hans Carvel, I give thee this ring — whilst thou carriest it upon that finger, thy wife shall never carnally be known by any other than thyself, without thy special knowledge and consent. Grammercy, quoth Hans Carvel, my Lord Devil, I renounce Mahomet, if ever it shall come off my finger. The devil vanished, as is his custom, and then Hans Carvel, full of joy awaking, found that his middle-finger was as far as it could reach within the what-do-you-call-it of his wife. I did forget to tell thee, how his wife, as soon as she had felt the finger there, said, in recoiling her buttocks. Off, yes, nay, tut, pish, tush, aye, lord, that is not the thing which should be put up in that place. With this Hans Carvel thought that some pilfering fellow was about to take the ring from him.

Is not this an infallible, and sovereign antidote? Therefore, if thou wilt believe me, in imitation of this example never fail to have continually the ring of thy wife's commodity upon thy finger.

Rabelais from *Gargantua and Pantagruel*
translated by Sir Thomas Urquhart

∾

Valentinian on women.

A common whore serves you, and far above ye,
The pleasures of a body lamed with lewdness;
 A mere perpetual motion makes ye happy
 . . . Your wanton jennets,
That are so proud the wind gets 'em with fillies,
Taught me this foul intemperance. Thou, Licinius,
Hast such a Messalina, such a Lais,
The backs of bulls cannot content, nor stallions;
The sweat of fifty men a-night does nothing.

John Fletcher from *Valentinian*

22 Now as they were making their hearts merry, behold, the men of the city, certain sons of Belial, beset the house round about, and beat at the door, and spake to the master of the house, the old man, saying, Bring forth the man that came into thine house, that we may know him.

23 And the man, the master of the house, went out unto them, and said unto them, Nay, my brethren, nay, I pray you, do not so wickedly; seeing that this man is come into mine house, do not this folly.

24 Behold, here is my daughter a maiden, and his concubine; them I will bring out now, and humble ye them, and do with them what seemeth good unto you: but unto this man do not so vile a thing.

25 But the men would not hearken to him: so the man took his concubine, and brought her forth unto them; and they knew her, and abused her all the night until the morning: and when the day began to spring, they let her go.

26 Then came the woman in the dawning of the day, and fell down at the door of the man's house where her lord was, till it was light.

27 And her lord rose up in the morning, and opened the doors of the house, and went out to go his way: and, behold, the woman his concubine was fallen down at the door of the house, and her hands were upon the threshold.

28 And he said unto her, Up, and let us be going. But none answered. Then the man took her up upon an ass, and the man rose up, and gat him unto his place.

29 And when he was come into his house, he took a knife, and laid hold on his concubine, and divided her, together with her bones, into twelve pieces, and sent her into all the coasts of Israel.

Judges 19

SIR JOLLY JUMBLE

The maw begins to empty. Get you before, and bespeak dinner at the Blue-Posts; while I stay behind and gather up a dish of whores for a dessert.

COURTINE

Be sure that they be lewd, drunken, stripping whores, Sir Jolly, that won't be affectedly squeamish and troublesome.

76

SOUR PUSS

SIR JOLLY JUMBLE
I warrant you.

COURTINE
I love a well-disciplined whore, that shows all the tricks of her profession with a wink, like an old soldier that understands all his exercises by beat of drum.

SIR JOLLY JUMBLE
Fail ye! am I a knight? hark ye, boys: I'll muster this evening such a regiment of rampant, roaring, roisterous whores, that shall make more noise than if all the cats in the Haymarket were in conjunction: whores, ye rogues, that shall swear with you, drink with you, talk bawdy with you, fight with you, scratch with you, lie with you, and go to the devil with you.

Thomas Otway from *The Soldier's Fortune*

Soranzo has discovered his newly-wed wife's adultery.

Come, strumpet, famous whore! were every drop
Of blood that runs in thy adulterous veins
A life, this sword — dost see't? should in one blow
Confound them all. Harlot, rare, notable harlot,
That with thy brazen face maintain'st thy sin,
Was there no man in Parma to be bawd
To your loose cunning whoredom else but I?

SOUR PUSS

Must your hot itch and plurisy of lust,
The heyday of your luxury, be fed
Up to a surfeit, and could none but I
Be pick'd out to be cloak to your close tricks,
Your belly-sports?

John Ford from *'Tis Pity She's a Whore*

❧

Thus finishing his grand survey,
The swain disgusted slunk away;
Repeating in his amorous fits,
'Oh! Caelia, Caelia, Caelia sh —!'

Jonathan Swift from 'The Lady's Dressing-Room'

To Each His Own

'I implore you, pity, pity, unloose me, unchain me, do not strike me so hard,' said a voice. 'I kiss your feet, I humiliate myself, I won't do it again, have pity' . . . And I heard the crack of a cat-o'-nine tails probably loaded with nails for it was followed by cries of pain . . . There on the bed, like Prometheus bound to his rock, squirming under the strokes of a cat-o'-nine tails, which was, as a matter of fact, loaded with nails, wielded by Maurice, already bleeding and covered with bruises, which proved he was not submitting to the torture for the first time, I saw before me M. de Charlus.

Marcel Proust from *Remembrance of Things Past*
translated by K. C. Scott-Moncrieff

❧

'Her perfume thrilled and stung him; he bent down and kissed her feet . . . which he took and pressed down upon his neck. "Oh! I should like you to tread me to death, darling . . . I wish you would kill me some day; it would be so jolly to feel you killing me. Not like it? Shouldn't I! You just hurt me and see." She pinched him so sharply that he laughed and panted with pleasure. "I should like being swished even I think, if you were to complain of me or if I knew you liked it." '

Algernon Swinburne from *Lesbia Brandon*

❧

TO EACH HIS OWN

... a pale chequer'd black hermaphrodite.
Sometimes he jets it like a gentleman,
Other whiles much like a wanton courtesan;
But, truth to tell, a man or woman whether,
I cannot say, she's excellent at either.

Thomas Middleton from Micro-Cynicon

Finally, up came a pansy, dressed in myrtle-green shaggy felt, which was tucked up under his belt. He pulled the cheeks of our bottoms apart, then he slobbered vile, greasy kisses on us, until Quartilla, carrying a whale-bone rod, with her skirts up round her, put an end to our sufferings.

Petronius from Satyricon
translated by John Sullivan

Bertie's tutor prepares him for Eton.

He tied the small wrists tight and laid on the lithe tough twigs with all the strength of his arm. There was a rage in him now more bitter than anger. The boy sobbed and flinched at each cut, feeling his eyes fill and blushing at his tears; but the cuts stung like fire, and burning with shame and pain alike, he pressed his hot wet face down on his hands, bit his sleeve, his fingers, anything: his teeth drew blood as well as the birch; he chewed the flesh of his hands rather than cry out, till Denham glittered with passion. A fresh rod was applied and he sang out sharply: then drew himself tight as it were all over, trying to brace his muscles and harden his flesh into rigid resistance; but the pain beat him; as he turned and raised his face, tears streamed over the inflamed cheeks and imploring lips. It was not the mere habit of sharp discipline, sense of official duty or flash of transient anger, that impelled his tormentor; had it been any of these he might have been more easily let off. As it was, Denham laid on every stripe with a cold fury that grew slowly to white heat; and when at length he made an end, he was seized with a fierce dumb sense of inner laughter; it was such an absurd relief this, and so slight. When these fits were on him he could have taken life to ease his bitter and wrathful despair of delight.

Algernon Swinburne from *Lesbia Brandon*

When Francus comes to solace with his whore,
He sends for rods and strips himself stark naked;
For his lust sleeps, and will not rise before
By whipping of the wench it be awaked.
I envy him not, but wish I had the power,
To make myself his wench but one half hour.

Christopher Marlowe from *Epigrames*

O lips full of lust and of laughter,
   Curled snakes that are fed from my breast,
Bite hard, lest remembrance come after
   And press with new lips where you pressed.
For my heart too springs up at the pressure,
   Mine eyelids too moisten and burn;
Ah, feed me and fill me with pleasure,
   Ere pain come in turn.

          *   *   *   *   *

Could you hurt me, sweet lips, though I hurt you?
   Men touch them, and change in a trice
The lilies and languors of virtue
   For the raptures and roses of vice;
Those lie where thy foot on the floor is,
   These crown and caress thee and chain,
O splendid and sterile Dolores,
   Our Lady of Pain.

          *   *   *   *   *

There are sins it may be to discover,
   There are deeds it may be to delight.
What new work wilt thou find for thy lover,
   What new passions for daytime or night?
What spells that they know not a word of
   Whose lives are as leaves overblown?
What tortures undreamt of, unheard of,
   Unwritten, unknown?

Algernon Swinburne from 'Dolores'

83

1 July 1663 . . . after dinner we fell in talking, Sir J. Mennes and Mr. Batten and I — Mr. Batten telling us of a late triall of Sir Charles Sydly the other day, before my Lord Chief Justice Foster and the whole Bench — for his debauchery a little while since at Oxford Kates; coming in open day into the Balcone and showed his nakedness — acting all the postures of lust and buggery that could be imagined, and abusing of scripture and, as it were, from thence preaching a Mountebanke sermon from that pulpitt, saying that there he hath to sell such a pouder as should make all the cunts in town run after him — a thousand people standing underneath to see and hear him.

And that being done, he took a glass of wine and washed his prick in it and then drank it off; and then took another and drank the King's health.

Samuel Pepys *Diary*

Denham looked her in the face, shaken inwardly and throughout by a sense of inevitable pain. . . . Rage rose in him again like a returning sea. . . . He would have given his life for leave to touch her; his soul for a chance of dying crushed down under her feet; an emotion of extreme tenderness, lashed to fierce insanity by the circumstance passed into a passion of vehement cruelty. Deeply he desired to die by her if that could be; and more deeply, if this could be, to destroy her; scourge her into swooning and absorb her blood with kisses; caress and lacerate her loveliness, alleviate and heighten her pains; to feel her foot upon his throat, and wound her own with his teeth; submit his body and soul for a little to her lightest will and satiate upon her the desperate caprice of his immeasurable desire; to inflict careful torture on the limbs too tender to embrace; suck the tears off her laden eyelids, bite through her sweet and shuddering lips.

Algernon Swinburne from *Lesbia Brandon*

84

Spectator Sports

She made a song, how little miss,
  Was kissed and slobber'd by a lad;
And how, when master went to p—s,
  Miss came, and peep'd at all he had.

Jonathan Swift from 'Corinna'

And all the margent round about was set,
With shady Laurell trees, thence to defend
The sunny beames, which on the billowes bet,
And those which therein bathed, mote offend.
As *Guyon* hapned by the same to wend,
Two naked Damzelles he therein espyde,
Which therein bathing, seemed to contend,
And wrestle wantonly, ne car'd to hyde,
Their dainty parts from vew of any, which them eyde.

Sometimes the one would lift the other quight
Aboue the waters, and then downe againe
Her plong, as ouer maistered by might,
Where both awhile would couered remaine,
And each the other from to rise restraine;
The whiles their snowy limbes, as through a vele,
So through the Christall waues appeared plaine:
Then suddeinly both would themselues vnhele,
And th'amarous sweet spoiles to greedy eyes reuele.

*   *   *   *   *

The wanton Maidens him espying, stood
Gazing a while at his vnwonted guise;
Then th'one her selfe low ducked in the flood,
Abasht, that her a straunger did a vise:
But th'other rather higher did arise,
And her two lilly paps aloft displayd,
And all, that might his melting hart entise
To her delights, she vnto him bewrayd:
The rest hid vnderneath, him more desirous made.

Edmund Spenser from *The Faerie Queene* (2. 12)

Being one Day abroad with my Protector the Sorrel Nag, and the
Weather exceeding hot, I entreated him to let me bathe in a
River that was near. He consented, and I immediately stripped
myself stark naked, and went down softly into the Stream. It
happened that a young Female *Yahoo* standing behind a Bank,
saw the whole Proceeding; and inflamed by Desire, as the Nag
and I conjectured, came running with all Speed, and leaped into
the Water within five Yards of the Place where I bathed. I was
never in my Life so terribly frighted; the Nag was grazing at some
Distance, not suspecting any Harm: She embraced me after a
most fulsome Manner; I roared as loud as I could, and the Nag
came galloping towards me, whereupon she quitted her Grasp,
with the utmost Reluctancy, and leaped upon the opposite
Bank, where she stood gazing and howling all the time I was
putting on my Cloaths.

Jonathan Swift from *Gulliver's Travels*

At night, when all they went to sleep, he vewd
Whereas his lovely wife emongst them lay,
Embraced of a Satyre rough and rude,
Who all the night did minde his joyous play:
Nine times he heard him come aloft ere day,
That all his heart with gelosy did swell;
But yet that night's ensample did bewray
That not for nought his wife them loved so well,
When one so oft a night did ring his matins bell.

Edmund Spenser from *The Faerie Queene* (3.10)

✺

BEAUGARD

Already a cuckold, Sir Jolly?

SIR JOLLY JUMBLE

No, that shall be, my boy; thou shalt make him one, and I'll pimp
for thee, dear heart; and shan't I hold the door? shan't I peep,
ha? shan't I, you devil, you little dog, shan't I?

BEAUGARD

What is it I'd not grant to oblige my patron?

SIR JOLLY JUMBLE

And then dost thou hear, I have a lodging for thee in my own
house: dost hear, old soul? in my own house; she lives the very
next door, man; there's but a wall to part her chamber and thine;
and then for a peep-hole — odd's fish, I have a peep hole for
thee; s'bud, I'll show thee, I'll show thee —

Thomas Otway from *The Soldier's Fortune*

Mary, Countesse of Pembroke, was sister to Sir Philip Sydney: maried to Henry, the eldest son of William Earle of Pembroke; but this subtile old Earle did see that his faire and witty daughter-in-lawe would horne his sonne, and told him so, and advised him to keepe her in the Countrey and not to let her frequent the Court.

She was a beautifull Ladie and had an excellent witt, and had the best breeding that that age could afford. Shee had a pritty sharpe-ovall face. Her haire was of a reddish yellowe.

She was very salacious, and she had a Contrivance that in the Spring of the yeare, when the Stallions were to leape the Mares, they were to be brought before such a part of the house, where she had a *vidette* (a hole to peepe out at) to looke on them and please herselfe with their Sport; and then she would act the like sport herselfe with *her* stallions. One of her great Gallants was Crooke-back't Cecill, Earl of Salisbury.

'Mary Herbert; Countess of Pembroke' from *Aubrey's Brief Lives* edited by Oliver Lawson Dick

DIPHILUS

Sister, Dula swears
She heard you cry two rooms off.

EVADNE

Fie, how you talk!

DIPHILUS

Let's see you walk.

Beaumont and Fletcher from *The Maid's Tragedy*

✼

Psyche had already put a veil round the girl's head and old Night-cap was leading the way with a torch. The tipsy women, still clapping, had formed a long line and had fixed up a bridal chamber with draperies in the appropriate sacrilegious way. Then Quartilla, highly excited by all this playful obscenity, rose to her feet herself, seized Giton, and dragged him into the chamber.

It was obvious the boy had not struggled and even the girl had not been dismayed or scared by the mention of marriage. And so, when they were shut in and lying down, we sat round the chamber doorway, and Quartilla was one of the first to put an inquisitive eye to a crack she had naughtily opened, and spy on their childish play with prurient eagerness. Her insistent hand pulled me down also to have a similar look, and since our faces were pressed together as we watched, whenever she could spare a moment, she would move her lips close to mine in passing and bruise me with sly kisses.

Petronius from *Satyricon*
translated by John Sullivan

Full on this casement shone the wintry moon,
And threw warm gules on Madeline's fair breast,
As down she knelt for heaven's grace and boon;
Rose-bloom fell on her hands, together prest,
And on her silver cross soft amethyst,
And on her hair a glory, like a saint:
She seem'd a splendid angel, newly drest,
Save wings, for heaven: — Porphyro grew faint:
She knelt, so pure a thing, so free from mortal taint.

Anon his heart revives: her vespers done,
Of all its wreathed pearls her hair she frees;
Unclasps her warmed jewels one by one;
Loosens her fragrant boddice; by degrees
Her rich attire creeps rustling to her knees
Half-hidden, like a mermaid in sea-weed,
Pensive awhile she dreams awake, and sees,
In fancy, fair St. Agnes in her bed,
But dares not look behind, or all the charm is fled.

          *   *   *   *   *

Stol'n to this paradise, and so entranced,
Porphyro gazed upon her empty dress,
And listen'd to her breathing, if it chanced
To wake into a slumberous tenderness;
Which when he heard, that minute did he bless,
And breath'd himself: then from the closet crept,
Noiseless as fear in a wide wilderness,
And over the hush'd carpet, silent, stept,
And 'tween the curtains peep'd, where, lo! — how fast she slept.

John Keats from *The Eve of St Agnes*

Oh listen, nymphs! in sunny wind,
Emily on the lawn reclined;
One of her beauteous arms was wound,
Embracingly her pillow round;
Her face and bosom, 'neath the sky,
Backwardly lolled in smiles did lie;
Her face and bosom upward bending
Flushed as with virgin shames; and lending
Her hand to some caressing dream,
Over her flowing limbs it lay,
Where stricken by the sunny beam,
Around it rosy lights did play:
And seemed those gently swelling limbs,
Curving at sound of warm love-hymns,
Towards fond minglement, though they
Minglement made not, but did stray
Partedly ever; — and the dress
Which fell soft o'er this loveliness,
Its glowing life all unconcealing,
Yet shaded from entire revealing —
With witching modesty, confessing
What matchless splendor still it veiled,
Though oft the breezes, rudely pressing,
The heavenly secrecy assailed, —
And then illumined the couch of azure,
And then the air did pant and glow,
While shivering with mysterious pleasure,
Like waves her limbs did lift and flow.

     *   *   *   *   *

Upon that ground her robe was spread,
And on that robe was lain my head;
Into its folds, burningly yearning,
My lips went, pouring kisses, till
I shook with ecstasy.
           Ebenezer Jones from 'Emily'

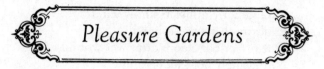

Pleasure Gardens

'Fondling', she saith, 'since I have hemmed thee here
Within the boundary of this ivory pale,
I'll be a park, and thou shalt be my deer:
Feed where thou wilt, on mountains or in dale.
    Graze on my lips — and if those hills be dry
    Stray lower, where the pleasant fountains lie.

'Within this limit is relief enough —
Sweet bottom-grass and high delightful plain,
Round rising hillocks, brakes obscure and rough,
To shelter thee from tempest and from rain.
    Then be my deer, since I am such a park.
    No dog shall rouse thee, though a thousand bark.'

William Shakespeare from Venus and Adonis

8 We have a little sister, and she
hath no breasts: what shall we do
for our sister in the day when she
shall be spoken for?
9 If she be a wall, we will build
upon her a palace of silver: and if
she be a door, we will inclose her
with boards of cedar.
10 I am a wall, and my breasts
like towers: then was I in his eyes
as one that found favour.

Song of Solomon 8

I do not love thee for those mountains
Hilled with snow, whence milky fountains
(Sugared sweets as syrup'd berries)
Must one day run through pipes of cherries;
O how much those breasts do move me!
Yet for them I do not love thee.

I do not love thee for that belly
Sleek as satin, soft as jelly,
Though within that crystal round
Heaps of treasure might be found,
So rich, that for the best of them,
A king might leave his diadem.

I do not love thee for those thighs,
Whose alabaster rocks do rise
So high and even, that they stand
Like sea-marks to some happy land:
Happy are those eyes have seen them;
More happy those that sail between them.

Thomas Carew from 'The Compliment'

Each man his humour hath, and faith 'tis mine
To love a woman which I now define.
First I would have her wainscot-foot and hand
More wrinkled far than any plaited band,
That in those furrows, if I'd take the pains,
I might both sow and reap all sorts of grains:
Her nose I'd have a foot long, not above,
With pimples embroidered, for those I love;

And at the end a comely pearl of snot,
Considering whether it should fall or not:
Provided, next, that half her teeth be out,
Nor do I care much if her pretty snout
Meet with her furrowed chin, and both together
Hem in her lips, as dry as good white leather.
One wall-eye she shall have; for that's a sign
In other beasts the best, why not in mine?
Her neck I'll have to be pure jet at least,
With yellow spots enamelled; and her breast,
Like a grasshopper's wing, both thin and lean,
Not to be touched for dirt, unless swept clean.
As for her belly, 'tis no matter so
There be a belly, and a c— — — also.
Yet if you will, let it be something high,
And always let there be a timpany —
But soft! where am I now? here I should stride,
Lest I fall in, the place must be so wide,
And pass unto her thighs, which shall be just
Like to an ant's that's scraping in the dust.
Into her legs I'd have love's issue fall,
And all her calf into a gouty small:
Her feet both thick and eagle-like displayed,
The symptoms of a comely, handsome maid.
As for her parts behind, I ask no more,
If they but answer those that are before,
I have my utmost wish; and having so,
Judge whether I am happy — yea or no.

Sir John Suckling from *The Deformed Mistress*

'I'm not sleepy; I'm not going to bed,' she said, when they were alone together.

The Count obeyed her with the meekness of a man no longer afraid of being seen. His only care was to avoid annoying her.

'Just as you wish,' he murmured.

All the same, he took his boots off too, before sitting down by the fire. One of Nana's pleasures consisted of undressing in front of the mirror on her wardrobe door, which reflected her from head to foot. She used to take off all her clothes and then stand stark naked, gazing at her reflection and oblivious of everything else around her. A passion for her body, an ecstatic admiration of her satin skin and the supple lines of her figure, kept her serious, attentive and absorbed in her love of herself. The hairdresser often found her standing like that, but she did not so much as turn her head as he came in. Muffat was always angry when this happened, much to her surprise. What had got into him? She did that to please herself, not other people.

*   *   *   *   *

. . . Nana had grown absorbed in her ecstatic contemplation of herself. She had bent her neck and was gazing attentively in the mirror at a little brown mole just above her right hip. She was touching it with the tip of her finger, and by leaning backwards was making it stand out more than ever; situated where it was, it presumably struck her as both quaint and pretty. Then she studied other parts of her body, amused by what she was doing, and filled once more with the depraved curiosity she had felt as a child. The sight of herself always surprised her, and she looked as astonished and fascinated as a young girl who has just discovered her puberty. Slowly she spread out her arms to set off her figure, the torso of a plump Venus, bending this way and that to examine herself in front and behind, lingering over the side-view of her bosom and the sweeping curves of her thighs. And she ended up by indulging in a strange game which consisted of swinging to right and left, with her knees apart, and

95

her body swaying from the waist with the continuous quivering
of an almeh performing a belly-dance.

Emile Zola from *Nana*
translated by George Holden

Then, as the empty bee that lately bore
Into the common treasure all her store
Flies 'bout the painted field with nimble wing
Deflowering the fresh virgins of the spring,
So will I rifle all the sweets that dwell
In my delicious paradise, and swell
My bag with honey drawn forth by the power
Of fervent kisses from each spicy flower;
I'll seize the rose-buds in their perfumed bed,
The violet knots like curious mazes spread
O'er all the garden; taste the ripened cherry,
The warm firm apple tipped with coral berry;
Then will I visit with a wandering kiss
The vale of lilies and the bower of bliss;
And where the beauteous region doth divide
Into two milky ways, my lips shall slide
Down those smooth alleys, wearing as I go
A tract for lovers on the printed snow;
Thence climbing o'er the swelling Apennine,
Retire into they grove of eglantine
Where I will all those ravished sweets distil
Through love's alembic, and with chemic skill
From the mixed mass one sovereign balm derive,
Then bring that great elixir to thy hive.

Thomas Carew from *A Rapture*

PLEASURE GARDENS

Hair, bosom, hips, bend of legs, negligent falling hands,
  all diffused — mine too diffused,
Ebb stung by the flow, and flow stung by the ebb,
  loveflesh swelling and deliciously aching,
Limitless limpid jets of love hot and enormous, quivering
  jelly of love, white-blow and delirious juice,
Bridegroom-night of love, working surely and safely into
  the prostrate dawn,
Undulating into the willing and yielding day,
Lost in the cleave of the clasping and sweet-fleshed day.

Walt Whitman from Leaves of Grass

₧

Off with that girdle, like heaven's Zone glistering,
But a far fairer world encompassing.
Unpin that spangled breastplate which you wear,
That th' eyes of busy fools may be stopt there.
Unlace yourself, for that harmonious chime
Tells me from you, that now it is bed time.
Off with that happy busk, which I envy,
That still can be, and still can stand so nigh.
Your gown going off, such beauteous state reveals,
As when from flowry meads th' hill's shadow steals.
Off with that wiry Coronet and show
The hairy Diadem which on you doth grow:
Now off with those shoes, and then safely tread
In this love's hallow'd temple, this soft bed.
In such white robes, heaven's Angels used to be
Receiv'd by men; thou Angel bring'st with thee
A heaven like Mahomet's Paradise; and though
Ill spirits walk in white, we easily know,

By this these Angels from an evil spirit,
Those set our hairs, but these our flesh upright.
   Licence my roving hands, and let them go,
Before, behind, between, above, below.
O my America! my new-found-land,
My kingdom, safeliest when with one man mann'd,
My Mine of precious stones, My Empery,
How blest am I in this discovering thee!
To enter in these bonds, is to be free;
Then where my hand is set, my seal shall be.

John Donne from 'To His Mistress Going to Bed'

5 Thy two breasts are like two
young roes that are twins, which
feed among the lilies.
12 A garden inclosed is my sister,
my spouse; a spring shut up, a
fountain sealed.
16 Awake, O north wind; and
come, thou south; blow upon my
garden, that the spices thereof
may flow out. Let my beloved
come into his garden, and eat his
pleasant fruits.

Song of Solomon 4

Hims to Venus

Each of us, then, is but a tally of a man, since every one shows like a flat-fish the traces of having been sliced in two; and each is ever searching for the tally that will fit him. All the men who are sections of that composite sex that at first was called man-woman are woman-courters; our adulterers are mostly descended from that sex, whence likewise are derived our man-courting women and adulteresses. All the women who are sections of the woman have no great fancy for men: they are inclined rather to women, and of this stock are the she-minions. Men who are sections of the male pursue the masculine, and so long as their boyhood lasts they show themselves to be slices of the male by making friends with men and delighting to lie with them and to be clasped in men's embraces; these are the finest boys and striplings, for they have the most manly nature. Some say they are shameless creatures, but falsely: for their behaviour is due not to shamelessness but to daring, manliness, and virility, since they are quick to welcome their like. Sure evidence of this is the fact that on reaching maturity these alone prove in a public career to be men. So when they come to man's estate they are boy-lovers, and have no natural interest in wiving and getting children, but only do these things under stress of custom; they are quite contented to live together unwedded all their days. A man of this sort is at any rate born to be a lover of boys or the willing mate of a man, eagerly greeting his own kind. Well, when one of them — whether he be a boy-lover or a lover of any other sort — happens on his own particular half, the two of them are wondrously thrilled with affection and intimacy and love, and are hardly to be induced to leave each other's side for a single moment.

Plato from *Symposium*
translated by H. Rackham

I do not press my finger across my mouth,
I keep as delicate around the bowels as around the head and
  heart,
Copulation is no more rank to me than death is.

I believe in the flesh and the appetites,
Seeing hearing and feeling are miracles, and each part and tag of
  me is a miracle.

Divine am I inside and out, and I make holy whatever I touch or
  am touched from;
The scent of these arm-pits is aroma finer than prayer,
This head is more than churches or bibles or creeds.

If I worship any particular thing it shall be some of the spread of
  my body;
Translucent mould of me it shall be you,
Shaded ledges and rests, firm masculine coulter, it shall be you,
Whatever goes to the tilth of me it shall be you,
You my rich blood, your milky stream pale strippings of my life;
Breast that presses against other breasts it shall be you,
My brain it shall be your occult convolutions,
Root of washed sweet-flag, timorous pond-snipe, nest of guarded
  duplicate eggs, it shall be you,
Mixed tussled hay of head and beard and brawn it shall be you,
Trickling sap of maple, fibre of manly wheat, it shall be you;
Sun so generous it shall be you,
Vapors lighting and shading my face it shall be you,
You sweaty brooks and dews it shall be you,
Winds whose soft-tickling genitals rub against me it shall be you,
Broad muscular fields, branches of liveoak, loving lounger in my
  winding paths, it shall be you,
Hands I have taken, face I have kissed, mortal I have ever
  touched, it shall be you.

                              Walt Whitman from *Leaves of Grass*

24 Wherefore God also gave them up to uncleanness through the lusts of their own hearts, to dishonour their own bodies between themselves:
25 Who changed the truth of God into a lie, and worshipped and served the creature more than the Creator, who is blessed for ever. Amen.
26 For this cause God gave them up unto vile affections: for even their women did change the natural use into that which is against nature:
27 And likewise also the men, leaving the natural use of the woman, burned in their lust one toward another; men with men working that which is unseemly, and receiving in themselves that recompence of their error which was meet.

Romans 1

Mankind is ruled by the Fates, they even govern those private
Parts that our clothes conceal. If your stars go against you
The fantastic size of your cock will get you precisely nowhere,
However much Virro may have drooled at the spectacle
Of your naked charms, though love-letters come by the dozen
Imploring your favours, though — quote — A man is attracted
By the very sight of — a pansy. Yet what could be lower
Than a close-fisted queer? 'I paid you so much then,'
He says, 'and a bit more later, and more that other time —'
Working it out by piece-rates. 'Well,' I say, 'fetch the accountant
With his reckoner and tables, tot up the total figure:
A miserable five thousand. Now list my services. Do you
Suppose it's easy, or fun, this job of cramming
My cock up into your guts till I'm stopped by last night's supper?
The slave who ploughs his master's field has less trouble
Than the one who ploughs him.'

Juvenal from *Satires*
translated by P. Green

101

MASKALL
And just now he showed me, how you were assaulted in the dark by foreigners.

LOPEZ
Could you guess what countrymen?

MASKALL
I imagined them to be Italians.

LOPEZ
Not unlikely; for they played most furiously at our backsides.

John Dryden from *The Mock Astrologer*

There is no soul so vile, no heart so barbarous as to be insusceptible to some sort of affection, and one of the two cut-throats who called themselves Moors took a fancy to me. He was fond of coming up to me and gossiping with me in his queer jargon. He did me little services, sometimes giving me some of his food at table, and he frequently kissed me with an ardour which I found most displeasing. But, frightened though I naturally was by his dusky face, which was beautified by a long scar, and by his passionate glances, which seemed to me more savage than affectionate, I put up with his kisses, saying to myself, 'The poor man has conceived a warm friendship for me; it would be wrong to repulse him.' But he passed by degrees to more unseemly conduct, and sometimes made me such strange suggestions that I thought he was wrong in the head. One night he wanted to share my bed, but I objected on the plea that it was too narrow. He then pressed me to come into his. I still refused, however, for the poor devil was so dirty and smelt so strongly of the tobacco he chewed that he made me feel ill.

102

Next day, very early in the morning, we were alone together in the assembly-hall. He resumed his caresses, but with such violence that I was frightened. Finally he tried to work up to the most revolting liberties and, by guiding my hand, to make me take the same liberties with him. I broke wildly away with a cry and leaped backwards, but without displaying indignation or anger, for I had not the slightest idea what it was all about. But I showed my surprise and disgust to such effect that he then left me alone. But as he gave up the struggle I saw something whitish and sticky shoot towards the fireplace and fall on the ground. My stomach turned over, and I rushed on to the balcony, more upset, more troubled and more frightened as well, than ever I had been in my life.

Jean-Jacques Rousseau from Confessions
translated by J. M. Cohen

✠

Geraldine, the beautiful stranger to whom Christabel has offered shelter for the night, begins to act very queerly.

> Again the wild-flower wine she drank:
> Her fair large eyes 'gan glitter bright,
> And from the floor whereon she sank,
> The lofty lady stood upright;
> She was most beautiful to see,
> Like a lady of a far countrée.
>
> And thus the lofty lady spake —
> All they, who live in the upper sky,
> Do love you, holy Christabel!
> And you love them, and for their sake
> And for the good which me befell,

103

Even I in my degree will try,
Fair maiden, to requite you well.
But now unrobe yourself; for I
Must pray, ere yet in bed I lie.

Quoth Christabel, so let it be!
And as the lady bade, did she.
Her gentle limbs did she undress,
And lay down in her loveliness.

But through her brain of weal and woe
So many thoughts moved to and fro,
That vain it were her lids to close;
So half-way from the bed she rose,
And on her elbow did recline
To look at the lady Geraldine.

Beneath the lamp the lady bowed,
And slowly rolled her eyes around;
Then drawing in her breath aloud
Like one that shuddered, she unbound
The cincture from beneath her breast:
Her silken robe, and inner vest,
Dropt to her feet, and full in view,
Behold! her bosom and half her side —
A sight to dream of, not to tell!
O shield her! shield sweet Christabel!

Yet Geraldine nor speaks nor stirs;
Ah! what a stricken look was hers!
Deep from within she seems half-way
To lift some weight with sick assay,
And eyes the maid and seeks delay;
Then suddenly as one defied
Collects herself in scorn and pride,
And lay down by the maiden's side! —

And in her arms the maid she took,
    Ah Well-a-day!
And with low voice and doleful look
These words did say:
In the touch of this bosom there worketh a spell,
Which is lord of thy utterance, Christabel!
Thou knowest to-night, and wilt know to-morrow
This mark of my shame, this seal of my sorrow;

    But vainly thou warrest,
      For this is alone in
    Thy power to declare,
      That in the dim forest
    Thou heard'st a low moaning,
And found'st a bright lady, surpassingly fair:
And didst bring her home with thee in love and in charity,
To shield her and shelter her from the damp air.

Samuel Taylor Coleridge from *Christabel*

A favourite Persian punishment for strangers caught in the Harem or Gynaeceum is to strip and throw them and expose them to the embraces of the grooms and negro slaves. I once asked a Shirazi how penetration was possible if the patient resisted with all the force of the sphincter muscle: he smiled and said, 'Ah, we Persians know a trick to get over that; we apply a sharpened tent-peg to the crupper bone (*os coccygis*) and knock till he opens'. A well known missionary to the East during the last generation was subjected to this gross insult by one of the Persian Prince-governors, whom he had infuriated by his conversion-mania: in his memoirs he alludes to it by mentioning his 'dishonoured person'; but English readers cannot comprehend the full significance of the confession. About the same time Shaykh Nasr, Governor of Bushire, a man famed for facetious blackguardism, used to invite European youngsters serving in the Bombay Marine and ply them with liquor till they were insensible. Next morning the middies mostly complained that the champagne had caused a curious irritation and soreness in *la parte-poste*.

Sir Richard Burton from Arabian Nights

❧

Dawn smiles on the fields of Eton, and wakes from slumber
   her youthful flock,
Lad by lad, whether good or bad: alas for those who at
   nine o'clock
Seek the room of disgraceful doom, to smart like fun on
   the flogging block.

Swish, swish, swish! O I wish, I wish I'd not been late
   for lock-up last night!
Swish, that mill I'm bruised from still (I couldn't help
   it — I had to fight)
Makes the beast (I suppose at least) who flogs me flog me
   with all his might.

'Tell me, S—e, does shame within burn as hot (Swish!
   Swish!) as your stripes my lad,
Burn outside, have I tamed your pride? I'm glad to see
   how it hurts you — glad —
Swish! I wish it may cure you. Swish! Get up.' By Jove,
   what a dose I've had.

Algernon Swinburne, song

'Splash me a little,' he cried, and the boys teased him with water and quite excited him. He chased the prettiest of them and bit his fesses, and kissed him upon the perineum till the dear fellow banded like a carmelite, and its little bald top-knot looked like a great pink pearl under the water. As the boy seemed anxious to take up the active attitude, Tannhauser graciously descended to the passive — a generous trait that won him the complete affections of his *valets de bain*, or pretty fish, as he liked to call them, because they loved to swim between his legs.

Aubrey Beardsley from *Under the Hill*

'It makes me feel very queer,' he said; 'it makes me feel —
queer!'

The Earl looked at the boy in silence. It made him feel queer
too — queerer than he had ever felt in his whole life. And he felt
more queer still when he saw that there was a troubled expression
on the small face which was usually so happy . . . .

Then he looked up at his grandfather, and there was a wistful
shade in his eyes, and they looked very big and soft.

'That other boy,' he said rather tremulously — 'he will have to
be your boy now — as I was — won't he?'

'No!' answered the Earl — and he said it so fiercely and loudly
that Cedric quite jumped. 'No?' he exclaimed in wonderment.
'Won't he? I thought —'

He stood up from his stool quite suddenly.

'Shall I be your boy, even if I'm not going to be an earl?' And
his flushed little face was all alight with eagerness.

How the old Earl did look at him from head to foot, to be sure!
How his great shaggy brows did draw themselves together, and
how queerly his deep eyes shone under them — how very
queerly!

'My boy!' he said — and, if you'll believe it, his very voice was
queer, almost shaky and a little broken and hoarse, not at all
what you would expect an earl's voice to be, though he spoke
more decidedly and peremptorily even than before — 'yes,
you'll be my boy as long as I live; and, by George, sometimes I
feel as if you were the only boy I had ever had.'

Cedric's face turned red to the roots of his hair . . .

Frances Hodgson Burnett from Little Lord Fauntleroy

ᕽ

In a letter to her friend Ermyntrude, Esmeralda describes
'a very extraordinary thing' that she overheard in the
Morning Room.

. . . what do you think I heard? You'll never guess — only I only
half heard it really, because it was so mumbling and indistinct
and it seemed so funny and extraordinary. I'm sure he was
making love. He kept on saying 'I love you more than anybody in
the world', and things like that, and 'Do you love me? Do you —
love me as much as I love you?' a great many times, and 'You're
the most beautiful creature in the world, how can you be so
beautiful?' and 'My dearest dearest dearest angel', and things
like that. Don't you think he must have been making love? Of
course I couldn't imagine who he was talking to, but I thought it
might be the under housemaid, who's quite pretty, but not the
most beautiful person in the world — but then people always do
exaggerate when they're making love, don't they — and then I
was just wondering whether perhaps it was Carrie, when
somebody else said 'Darling — darling' — just like that, and my
dear, it was Godfrey! That gave me such a jump that I very nearly
dropped all my books — the grammar and dictionary and
everything — but I luckily didn't, and by that time the room
seemed rather lighter and I made out that Godfrey's voice must
have come from behind a screen there is going across, so I
stretched out as far as I could, and just managed to see round the
screen to the sofa. And Mr. Mapleton was there too, with his arm
round Godfrey's neck, and they were kissing and their hair was
all tousled, but the most extraordinary thing of all was that their
buttons were so much undone that their shirts were all coming
out. Wasn't it too peculiar for words?

Lytton Strachey from *Ermyntrude and Esmeralda*

A conversation between two schoolboys.

'You know what the young knights were taught, Monty — to keep their bodies under, and bring them into subjection; to love God, and speak the truth always. That sounds very grand and noble to me. But when a big fellow takes up a little one you know pretty well that *those* are not the kind of lessons he teaches.'

Frederic William Farrar from Eric, or Little by Little

❦

'Do you know any thing of my cousin's captain?' said Edmund; 'Captain Marshall? You have a large acquaintance in the navy, I conclude?'

'Among Admirals, large enough; but,' with an air of grandeur; 'we know very little of the inferior ranks. Post captains may be very good sort of men, but they do not belong to *us*. Of various admirals, I could tell you a great deal; of them and their flags, and the gradation of their pay, and their bickerings and jealousies. But in general, I can assure you that they are all passed over, and all very ill used. Certainly, my home at my uncle's brought me acquainted with a circle of admirals. Of *Rears*, and *Vices*, I saw enough. Now, do not be suspecting me of a pun, I entreat.'

Edmund again felt grave, and only replied, 'It is a noble profession.'

Jane Austen from Mansfield Park

❦

A woman's face, with Nature's own hand painted,
Hast thou, the master-mistress of my passion;
A woman's gentle heart, but not acquainted
With shifting change, as is false women's fashion;
An eye more bright than theirs, less false in rolling,
Gilding the object whereupon it gazeth;
A man in hew all *Hews* in his controlling,
Which steals men's eyes, and women's souls
   amazeth.
And for a woman were thou first created;
Till Nature, as she wrought thee, fell a-doting,
And by addition me of thee defeated,
By adding one thing to my purpose nothing.
  But since she prick'd thee out for women's
    pleasure,
  Mine be thy love, and thy love's use their
    treasure.

William Shakespeare from Sonnets

❦

One of the girls, a stranger to me, sat down at the piano, and Andrée invited Albertine to waltz with her. Happy in the thought that I was going to remain in this little casino with these girls, I remarked to Cottard how well they danced together. But he, taking the professional point of view of a doctor and with an ill-breeding which overlooked the fact that they were my friends, although he must have seen me shaking hands with them, replied: 'Yes, but parents are very rash to allow their daughters to form such habits. I should certainly never let mine come here. Are they nice-looking, though? I can't see their faces. There now, look,' he went on, pointing to Albertine and Andrée who were waltzing slowly, tightly clasped together, 'I have left my glasses behind and I don't see very well, but they are certainly keenly

111

roused. It is not sufficiently known that women derive most excitement from their breasts. And theirs' as you see, are completely touching.'

Marcel Proust from *Remembrance of Things Past*
translated by K. C. Scott-Moncrieff

☙

From this time Eric was much in Upton's study, and constantly by his side in the playground. In spite of their disparity in age and position in the school, they became sworn friends, though their friendship was broken every now and then by little quarrels, which united them all the more closely after they had not spoken to each other for a week.

Frederic William Farrar from *Eric, or Little by Little*

☙

No dream disturbed him. There was only an infinitely pleasant warmth spreading soft carpets under his body. After a while he woke out of it. And then he almost screamed. There, sitting on his bed, was Basini! And in the next instant, with crazy speed, Basini had flung off his night-clothes and slid under the blankets and was pressing his naked, trembling body against Törless.

As soon as Törless recovered from the shock, he pushed Basini away from him.

'What do you think you're doing − ?'

But Basini pleaded. 'Oh, don't start being like that again! Nobody's the way you are! They don't despise me the way you do. They only pretend they do, so as to be different then

112

afterwards. But you — you of all people! You're even younger than me, even if you are stronger. We're both younger than the others. You don't boast and bully the way they do . . . You're gentle . . . I love you . . .'

'Here, I say! I don't know what you're talking about! I don't know what you want! Go away! Oh, go *away*!' And in anguish Törless pushed his arm against Basini's shoulder, holding him off. But the hot proximity of the soft skin, this other person's skin, haunted him, enclosing him, suffocating him. And Basini kept on whispering: 'Oh yes . . . oh yes . . . please . . . oh, I should so gladly do whatever you want!'

Robert Musil from Young Törless
translated by Kaiser and Wilkins

❧

'I'd rather have gone to Madame Robert's,' said Satin. 'There's always a corner there for me. . . . But with you that's out of the question. She's getting so jealous it's quite ridiculous; she beat me the other night.'

When they had locked themselves in, Nana who had not yet relieved her feelings, burst into tears and recounted over and over again the dirty trick Fontan had played on her. Satin listened indulgently, comforting her and railing against the male sex even more indignantly than her friend.

'Oh, the swine, the swine! . . . We'll have nothing more to do with them, that's what we'll do!'

Then she helped Nana undress with all the gentle attentions of an adoring and submissive lover. She kept saying coaxingly:

'Let's go straight to bed, pet. We'll be better off there. . . . Oh, how silly you are to get all worked up! I tell you, they're dirty swine! Forget about them. . . . I'm here, and I love you. Don't cry now — just to please your little darling.'

And, once in bed, she took Nana in her arms straight away to comfort her. She refused to hear Fontan's name mentioned again, and every time it returned to her friend's lips, she stopped it with a kiss, pouting in pretty indignation, her hair lying loosely on the pillow, and her face full of tender, childlike beauty. Little by little her gentle embrace persuaded Nana to dry her tears. She was touched, and returned Satin's caresses. When two o'clock struck the candle was still burning, and the sound of muffled laughter was mingling with words of love.

Emile Zola from *Nana*
translated by George Holden

Family Ties

11 And the man that lieth with his father's wife hath uncovered his father's nakedness: both of them shall surely be put to death; their blood shall be upon them.

12 And if a man lie with his daughter in law, both of them shall surely be put to death: they have wrought confusion; their blood shall be upon them.

13 If a man also lie with mankind, as he lieth with a woman, both of them have committed an abomination: they shall surely be put to death; their blood shall be upon them.

14 And if a man take a wife and her mother, it is wickedness: they shall be burnt with fire, both he and they; that there be no wickedness among you.

15 And if a man lie with a beast, he shall surely be put to death: and ye shall slay the beast.

16 And if a woman approach unto any beast, and lie down thereto, thou shalt kill the woman, and the beast: they shall surely be put to death; their blood shall be upon them.

17 And if a man shall take his sister, his father's daughter, or his mother's daughter, and see her nakedness, and she see his nakedness; it is a wicked thing; and they shall be cut off in the sight of their people: he hath uncovered his sister's nakedness; he shall bear his iniquity.

18 And if a man shall lie with a woman having her sickness, and shall uncover her nakedness; he hath discovered her fountain, and she hath uncovered the fountain of her blood: and both of them shall be cut off from among their people.

19 And thou shalt not uncover the nakedness of thy mother's sister, nor of thy father's sister: for he uncovereth his near kin: they shall bear their iniquity.

20 And if a man shall lie with his uncle's wife, he hath uncovered his uncle's nakedness: they shall bear their sin; they shall die childless.

21 And if a man shall take his brother's wife, it is an unclean thing: he hath uncovered his brother's nakedness; they shall be childless.

Leviticus 20

Young Bertie wrestles at bedtime with his much older sister.

'I say, let your hair go,' said Herbert, pressing his arms under hers: she loosened the fastenings, and it rushed downwards, a tempest and torrent of sudden tresses, heavy and tawny and riotous and radiant, over shoulders and arms and bosom; and under cover of the massive and luminous locks she drew up his face against her own and kissed him time after time with all her strength.

'Now got to bed, and sleep well,' she said, putting him back. His whole spirit was moved with the passionate motion of his senses; he clung to her for a minute, and rose up throbbing from head to foot with violent love. All the day's pleasure and pain came suddenly to flower and bore fruit in him at the moment.

Algernon Swinburne from *Lesbia Brandon*

For according to Valande's wicked counsel and to his abominable pleasure which they mistakenly held to be their own, in that same night the brother slept with the sister as man with wife, and their chamber above in the donjon keep, round which the owls circled, was so full of tenderness, defilement, rage, and blood and sin that my heart turns over for pity, shame, and anguish and I may scarcely tell it all.

They both lay naked under their covers of soft sable in the pale gleam of the swinging lamp and the scent of the amber with which their beds were dusted — they stood, as fittingly, far apart, and between them, coiled round like a snake, slumbered Hanegiff, their good hound. But they could not sleep, they lay with open eyes or only sometimes shut them perforce. How it was with the damsel I do not know, but Wiligis, o'er-wrought by his father's death and his own life, groaned under the scourge of the flesh and under Valande's spur until at last he held out no longer and slipped out of his bed, went round Hanegiff on his bare foot soles, gently lifted Sibylla's cover and came, the godforsaken one, with a thousand forbidden kisses, to his sister.

She spoke jestingly, albeit with voice unjestingly choked:

'Lo, my Lord Duke, mickle honour you show me with your unexpected visit! What gives me the privilege of feeling your dear skin near mine? A joy would that be to me, if only round the tower the little owlets would not so awfully screech.'

'They always screech.'

'But not so awfully. That may be why your hands cannot rest but must so strangely wrestle with me. What means, my brother, this wrestling? How have I thy sweet shoulder at my lips? Why not? It is dear to me. Only you must not aim to part my knees one from the other; for they shall altogether and unconditionally remain together.'

Thomas Mann from *The Holy Sinner*
translated by H. T. Lowe-Porter

Antoninus Caracalla observed his mother-in-law with her breasts amorously laid open, he was so much moved, that he said, *Ah! si liceret!* Oh that I might! which she by chance over-hearing, replied as impudently, *Quicquid libet licet,* thou mayest do what thou wilt. And upon that temptation he married her: this object was not in cause, not the thing itself, but that unseemly, undecent carriage of it.

Robert Burton from *The Anatomy of Melancholy*

❧

QUEEN
O Hamlet, speak no more:
Thou turn'st mine eyes into my very soul;
And there I see such black and grained spots
As will not leave their tinct.

HAMLET
Nay, but to live
In the rank sweat of an enseamed bed,
Stew'd in corruption, honeying and making love
Over the nasty sty, —

QUEEN
O, speak to me no more;
These words, like daggers, enter in mine ears;
No more, sweet Hamlet!

William Shakespeare from *Hamlet*

❧

118

In his *Utopia* his lawe is that the young people are to see each other stark-naked before marriage. Sir William Roper, of Eltham, in Kent, came one morning, pretty early, to my Lord, with a proposall to marry one of his daughters. My Lord's daughters were then both together abed in a truckle-bed in their father's chamber asleep. He carries Sir William into the chamber and takes the Sheete by the corner and suddenly whippes it off. They lay on their Backs, and their smocks up as high as their arme-pitts. This awakened them, and immediately they turned on their bellies. Quoth Roper, I have seen both sides, and so gave a patt on the buttock, he made choice of, sayeing, Thou art mine. Here was all the trouble of the wooeing. This account I had from my honoured friend old Mris Tyndale, whose grandfather, Sir William Stafford, was an intimate friend of this Sir W. Roper, who told him the story.

'Sir Thomas More' from *Aubrey's Brief Lives*
edited by Oliver Lawson Dick

30 And Lot went up out of Zoar, and dwelt in the mountain, and his two daughters with him; for he feared to dwell in Zoar: and he dwelt in a cave, he and his two daughters.
31 And the firstborn said unto the younger, Our father is old, and there is not a man in the earth to come in unto us after the manner of all the earth:
32 Come, let us make our father drink wine, and we will lie with him, that we may preserve seed of our father.
33 And they made their father drink wine that night: and the firstborn went in, and lay with her father; and he perceived not when she lay down, nor when she arose.
34 And it came to pass on the morrow, that the firstborn said unto the younger, Behold, I lay yesternight with my father: let us make him drink wine this night also; and go thou in, and lie with him, that we may preserve seed of our father.
35 And they made their father drink wine that night also: and the younger arose, and lay with

him; and he perceived not when she lay down, nor when she arose.

36 Thus were both the daughters of Lot with child by their father.

37 And the firstborn bare a son, and called his name Moab: the same is the father of the Moabites unto this day.

Genesis 19

Animal Magic

And there are, also, lustful and chaste fishes; of which I shall give you examples.

And first, what Du Bartas says of a fish called the Sargus; which, because none can express it better than he does, I shall give you in his own words, supposing it shall not have the less credit for being verse; for he hath gathered this and other observations out of authors that have been great and industrious searchers into the secrets of nature.

> *The adult'rous Sargus doth not only change*
> *Wives every day in the deep streams, but, strange!*
> *As if the honey of sea-love delight*
> *Could not suffice his ranging appetite,*
> *Goes courting she-goats on the grassy shore,*
> *Horning their husbands that had horns before.*

And the same author writes concerning the Cantharus, that which you shall also hear in his own words.

> *But, contrary, the constant Cantharus*
> *Is ever constant to his faithful spouse;*
> *In nuptial duties, spending his chaste life;*
> *Never loves any but his own dear wife.*

Izaak Walton from *The Compleat Angler*

Concerning Deer there also passeth another opinion, that the Males thereof do yearly lose their pizzel. For men observing the decidence of their horns, do fall upon the like conceit of this part, that it annually rotteth away, and successively reneweth again. Now the ground hereof was surely the observation of this part in Deer after immoderate venery, and about the end of their Rut, which sometimes becomes so relaxed and pendulous, it cannot be quite retracted: and being often beset with flies, it is conceived to rot, and at last to fall from the body.

Sir Thomas Browne from *Pseudodoxia Epidemica*

That whale of Stubb's, so dearly purchased, was duly brought to the Pequod's side, where all those cutting and hoisting operations previously detailed, were regularly gone through, even to the baling of the Heidelburgh Tun, or Case.

While some were occupied with this latter duty, others were employed in dragging away the larger tubs, so soon as filled with the sperm; and when the proper time arrived, this same sperm was carefully manipulated ere going to the try-works, of which anon.

It had cooled and crystallized to such a degree, that when, with several others, I sat down before a large Constantine's bath of it, I found it strangely concreted into lumps, here and there rolling about in the liquid part. It was our business to squeeze these lumps back into fluid. A sweet and unctuous duty! No wonder that in old times sperm was such a favorite cosmetic. Such a clearer! such a sweetener! such a softener; such a delicious mollifier! After having my hands in it for only a few minutes, my fingers felt like eels, and began, as it were, to serpentine and spiralize.

As I sat there at my ease, cross-legged on the deck; after the

ANIMAL MAGIC

bitter exertion at the windlass; under a blue tranquil sky; the ship under indolent sail, and gliding so serenely along; as I bathed my hands among those soft, gentle globules of infiltrated tissues, wove almost within the hour; as they richly broke to my fingers, and discharged all their opulence, like fully ripe grapes their wine; as I snuffed up that uncontaminated aroma, — literally and truly, like the smell of spring violets; I declare to you, that for the time I lived as in a musky meadow . . .

Squeeze! squeeze! squeeze! all the morning long; I squeezed that sperm till I myself almost melted into it; I squeezed that sperm till a strange sort of insanity came over me; and I found myself unwittingly squeezing my co-laborers' hands in it, mistaking their hands for the gentle globules. Such an abounding, affectionate, friendly, loving feeling did this avocation beget; that at last I was continually squeezing their hands, and looking up into their eyes sentimentally; as much as to say, — Oh! my dear fellow beings, why should we longer cherish any social acerbities, or know the slightest ill-humor or envy! Come; let us squeeze hands all round; nay, let us all squeeze ourselves into each other; let us squeeze ourselves universally into the very milk and sperm of kindness.

Herman Melville from *Moby Dick*

᪐

Aphrodisiacs are: an application of wild-boar's gall, pig's marrow swallowed, or an application of ass's suet mixed with a gander's grease; also the fluid that Virgil too describes as coming from a mare after copulation, the testicles of a horse, dried so that they may be powdered into drink, the right testis of an ass taken in wine, or a portion of it worn as an amulet on a bracelet; or the foam of an ass after copulation, collected in a red cloth and enclosed, as Osthanes tells us, in silver. Salpe prescribes an ass's genital organ to be plunged seven times into hot oil, and the relevant parts to be rubbed therewith, the ash from it to be taken

123

in drink, or the urine of a bull after copulation to be drunk, or the mud itself made by it applied to the pubic parts. On the other hand antaphrodisiac for men is an application of mouse's dung.

Pliny from *Natural History*
translated by W. H. S. Jones

Calf's gall also, sprinkled on the uterus during menstruation just before intercourse, softens even indurations of the bowels, checks the flow if rubbed on the navel, and is generally beneficial to the uterus . . . If women about the time of conception eat roasted veal with aristolochia, they are assured that they will bring forth a male child. A calf's marrow, boiled down in wine and water with calf's suet and applied to an ulcerated uterus, is beneficial, as is the fat of foxes with the excrement of cats, the last being applied with resin and rose oil. It is thought that to fumigate the uterus with goat's horn is very beneficial.

Pliny from *Natural History*
translated by W. H. S. Jones

Moses issued a prohibition against eating the hare. The hare is forever mounting the female, leaping upon her crouching form from behind. In fact, this manner of having intercourse is a characteristic of the hare. The female conceives every month, and, even before the first offspring is born, she become pregnant again. She conceives and begets, and as soon as she gives birth is fertilized again by the first hare she meets. Not satisfied with one mate, she conceives again, although she is still nursing. The explanation is that the female hare has a double womb, and therefore her desire for intercourse is stimulated not only by the emptiness of the womb, in that every empty space seeks to be filled, but also, when she is with young, her other womb begins to feel lustful desires. That is why hares have one birth after the other. So the mysterious prohibition [of Moses] in reality is but counsel to restrain violent sexual impulses, and intercourse in too frequent succession, relations with a pregnant woman, pederasty, adultery, and lewdness.

Clement of Alexandria from *The Instructor*
translated by Simon P. Wood

Ktesias of Knidos is obviously mistaken in his statement about the semen of elephants: he says that it gets so hard when it solidities that it becomes like amber. It does not. It is, of course, true that one semen must of necessity be earthier than another, and the earthiest will be in those animals which, for their bodily bulk, contain a large amount of earthy matter; but semen is thick and white because there is *pneuma* mixed with it. What is more, it is white in all cases. Herodotus is incorrect when he says that the semen of Ethiopians is black, as though everything about a person with a black skin were bound to be black — and this too in spite of their teeth being white, as he could see for himself. The cause of the whiteness of semen is that it is foam, and foam is white, the whitest being that which consists of the tiniest particles, so small that each individual bubble cannot be detected by the eye. An instance of such a foam, mentioned earlier, is that produced by the mechanical mixing of water and oil.

That the natural substance of semen is foam-like was, so it seems, not unknown even in early days; at any rate, the goddess who is supreme in matters of sexual intercourse was called after foam.

We have now given the reason which solves the puzzle that was stated. And this also shows, incidentally, why semen does not freeze: it is because air is impervious to frost.

Aristotle from *Generation of Animals*
translated by A. L. Peck

Osthanes says that if the loins of a woman are rubbed thoroughly with the blood of a tick from a black wild-bull, she will be disgusted with sexual intercourse, and also with her love if she drinks the urine of a he-goat, nard being added to disguise the foul taste.

Pliny from *Natural History*
translated by W. H. S. Jones

His Antagonist, Dr Price the Anniversarist, was made Deane of Hereford. Dr Watts, Canon of that church, told me that this Deane was a mighty Pontificall proud man, and that one time when they went in Procession about the Cathedral church, he would not doe it the usually way in his surplice, hood, etc, on foot, but rode on a mare thus habited, with the Common prayer booke, in his hand, reading. A stone horse [stallion] happend to breake loose, and smelt the mare, and ran and leapt her, and held the Reverend Deane all the time so hard in his Embraces, that he could not gett off till the horse had done his bussinesse. But he would never ride in procession afterwards.

'Richard Corbet' from Aubrey's Brief Lives
edited by Oliver Lawson Dick

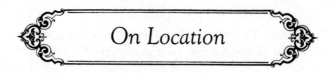

On Location

10 May 1763 At the bottom of the Haymarket I picked up a strong, jolly young damsel, and taking her under the arm I conducted her to Westminster Bridge, and then in armour complete did I engage her upon this noble edifice. The whim of doing it there with the Thames rolling below us amused me much. Yet after the brutish appetite was sated, I could not but despise myself for being so closely united with such a low wretch.

James Boswell *Journals*

May persuades her blind old husband, January, to give her a leg up into the pear tree where her lover is waiting.

'Certes,' quod he, 'theron shal be no lak,
Mighte I yow helpen with myn herte-blood.'
He stoupeth doun and on his bak she stood
And caughte hir by a twiste and vp she goth.
Ladys, I pray yow that ye be nat wroth:
I kan nat glose I, a rude man.
And sodeynly anon this Damyan
Gan pullen vp the smok and in he throng.

Geoffrey Chaucer from *The Merchant's Tale*

128

Dermot
No more that brier thy tender leg shall rake:
(I spare the thistle for Sir Arthur's sake).
Sharp are the stones; take thou this rushy mat;
The hardest bum will bruise with sitting squat.

Sheelah
Thy breeches, torn behind, stand gaping wide;
This petticoat shall save thy dear backside;
Nor need I blush, although you feel it wet,
Dermot, I vow, 'tis nothing else but sweat.

Jonathan Swift from 'Pastoral Dialogue'

At Berkeley in Gloucester-shire, there was in times past a
Nunnery (saith Gualterus Mapes, an old Historiographer, that
lived 400 years since) of which there was a noble and a fair Lady
Abbess: Godwin, that subtil Earl of Kent travelling that way
(seeking not her but hers) leaves a Nephew of his, a proper
young Gallant (as if he had been sick) with her, till he came back
again, and gives the young man charge so long to counterfeit, till
he had deflowered the Abbess, and as many besides of the Nuns
as he could, and leaves him withal rings, jewels, girdles, and such
toys to give them still, when they came to visit him. The young
man willing to undergo such a business, played his part so well,
that in short space he got up most of their bellies, and when he
had done, told his Lord how he had sped; his Lord makes
instantly to the Court, tells the King how such a Nunnery was
become a bawdy house, procures a visitation, gets them to be
turned out, and begs the lands to his own use.

Robert Burton from *The Anatomy of Melancholy*

LADY DUPE
... Good my lord, where was this wicked act then first committed?

LORD DARTMOUTH
In an out-room upon a trunk.

LADY DUPE
Poor heart, what shifts love makes! Oh! she does love you dearly, though to her ruin! And then, what place, my lord?

LORD DARTMOUTH
An old waste-room, with a decayed bed in't.

LADY DUPE
Out upon that dark room for deeds of darkness! And that rotten bed! I wonder it did hold your lordship's vigour.

John Dryden from *Sir Martin Marall*

❧

25 March 1668 Thence walked a little to Westminster, but met with nobody to spend any time with; and so by coach homeward, and in Seething-lane met young Mrs. Daniel, and I stopped; and she had been at my house but found nobody within, and tells me that she drew me for her valentine this year; so I took her into the coach, and was going to the other end of the town with her, thinking to have taken her abroad; but remembering that I was to go out with my wife this afternoon, I only did hazer her para tocar my prick con her hand, which did hazer me hazer; and so to a milliner at the corner shop going into Bishopsgate and Leadenhall-street, and there did give her eight pair of gloves, and so dismissed her; and so I home and to dinner.

Samuel Pepys *Diary*

Rowlandson del.

Absolon has been pestering Alison to let him kiss her. In the dead of night, she offers him not her face but her buttocks.

The wyndow she vndooth and that in haste.
'Haue do,' quod she, 'com of and speed thee faste
Lest that oure neghebores thee espye.'
This Absolon gan wipe his mouth ful drye.
Derk was the nyght as pych or as the cole,
And at the wyndow out she putte hir hole.
And Absolon hym fil no bet ne wers
But with his mouth he kiste hir naked ers
Ful sauourly, er he were war of this.
Abak he sterte and thoghte it was amys,
For wel he wiste a womman hath no berd.
He felte a thyng al rogh and longe yherd
And seyde: 'Fy allas, what haue I do?'
'Te-hee,' quod she, and clapte the wyndow to.

Geoffrey Chaucer from *The Miller's Tale*

❧

16 January 1664 I by water to Westminster Hall and there did see Mrs Lane and de là, elle and I to the cabaret at the Cloche in the street du Roy; and there, after some caresses, je l'ay foutée sous de la chaise deux times, and the last to my great pleasure; mais j'ai grand peur que je l'ay fait faire aussi elle même. Mais after I had done, elle commençait parler as before and I did perceive that je n'avais fait rien de danger à elle. Et avec ça, I came away; and though I did make grand promises à la contraire, nonobstant je ne la verrai pas long time. So home to supper and to bed —

132

with my mind un peu troublé pour ce que j'ai fait today. But I hope it will be la dernière de toute my vie . . .

Samuel Pepys *Diary*

❧

He loved a wench well; and one time getting up one of the Mayds of Honour up against a tree in a Wood ('twas his first Lady) who seemed at first boarding to be something fearfull of her Honour, and modest, she cryed, sweet Sir Walter, what doe you me ask; Will you undoe me? Nay, sweet Sir Walter! Sweet Sir Walter! Sir Walter! At last, as the danger and the pleasure at the same time grew higher, she cryed in the extasey, Swisser Swatter Swisser Swatter. She proved with child, and I doubt not but this Hero tooke care of them both, as also that the Product was more than an ordinary mortal.

'Sir Walter Raleigh' from *Aubrey's Brief Lives*
edited by Oliver Lawson Dick

133

Tailpieces

And is this all, is this (She cry'd)
Man's great Desire, and Woman's Pride;
The Spring whence flows the Lover's Pain,
The Ocean where 'tis lost again,
By Fate for ever doom'd to prove
The Nursery and grave of Love?
O Thou of dire and horrid Mien,
And always better felt than seen!
Fit Rapture of the gloomy Night,
O, never more approach the Light!
Like other Myst'ries Men adore,
Be hid, to be rever'd the more.

Hildebrand Jacob 'The Curious Maid'

To wonder sadly, did I say? No: a new influence began to act upon my life, and sadness, for a certain space, was held at bay. Conceive a dell, deep-hollowed in forest secrecy; it lies in dimness and mist: its turf is dank, its herbage pale and humid. A storm or an axe makes a wide gap amongst the oak trees; the breeze sweeps in; the sun looks down; the sad, cold dell becomes a deep cup of lustre; high summer pours her blue glory and her golden light out of that beauteous sky, which till now the starved hollow never saw.

Charlotte Bronte from *Villette*

134

The tailor thought to please her,
With offering her his measure.
The tinker too with mettle,
Said he could mend her kettle,
    And stop up every leak.

    *   *   *   *   *

The sailor slily waiting,
Thought if it came about, sir,
That they should all fall out, sir,
    He then might play his part.

    *   *   *   *   *

And then let fly at her
A shot 'twixt wind and water,
    That won this fair maid's heart.

William Congreve, a song from *Love for Love*

And in what modes the intercourse goes on, is likewise of very great moment; for women are commonly thought to conceive more readily after the manner of wild-beasts and quadrupeds, because the seeds in this way can find the proper spots, in consequence of the position of the body. Nor have wives the least use for effeminate motions: a woman hinders and stands in the way of her own conceiving, when thus she acts; for she drives the furrow out of the direct course and path of the share and turns away from the proper spots the stroke of the seed. And thus for their own ends harlots are wont to move, in order not to conceive and lie in child-bed frequently, and at the same time to render Venus more attractive to men.

Lucretius from *De Rerum Natura*
translated by H. A. J. Munro

Whence did all that fury come?
From empty tomb or Virgin womb?
Saint Joseph thought the world would melt
But liked the way his finger smelt.

W. B. Yeats 'A Stick of Incense'

I found nobody at home but my charming Fotis who was preparing pork-rissoles for her master and mistress, while the appetizing smell of haggis-stew drifted to my nostrils from an earthenware casserole on the stove. She wore a neat white housedress, gathered in below the breasts with a red silk band,

and as she alternately stirred the casserole and shaped the rissoles with her pretty hands, the twisting and turning made her whole body quiver seductively.

The sight had so powerful an effect on me that for awhile I stood rooted in admiration; and so did something else. At last I found my voice. 'Dear Fotis' I said, 'how daintily, how charmingly you stir that casserole: I love watching you wriggle your hips. And what a wonderful cook you are! The man whom you allow to poke his finger into your little casserole is the luckiest fellow alive. That sort of stew would tickle the most jaded palate.'

Apuleius from *The Golden Ass*
translated by Robert Graves

No public business of any kind could possibly be done at any time, without the acquiescence of the Circumlocution Office. Its finger was in the largest public pie, and in the smallest public tart.

Charles Dickens from *Little Dorrit*

On his wedding night the impotent Hans is helped out by the devil.

Hans took the ring with joy extreme —
All this was only in a dream —
And thrusting it beyond his joint,
' 'Tis done,' he cried, 'I've gained my point —'

137

'What point,' said she, 'you ugly beast?
You neither give me joy nor rest:
'Tis done — What's done, you drunken bear?
You've thrust your finger God knows where!'

Matthew Prior from 'Hans Carvel'

❧

And trewely as myne housbondes tolde me
I hadde the beste quonyam myghte be:
Myn ascendent was Taur and Mars therinne;
Allas, allas that euere loue was synne.
I folwed ay myn inclinacioun
By vertu of my constellacioun
That made me I koude noght withdrawe
My chambre of Venus from a good felawe.

Geoffrey Chaucer from *Wife of Bath's Prologue*

❧

Because the hyena is of all animals the most sensual, there is a knob of flesh underneath its tail, in front of the anus, closely resembling the female sex organ in shape. It is not a passage, I mean it serves no useful purpose, opening neither into the womb nor into the intestines. It has only a good-sized opening to permit an ineffective sexual act when the vagina is preparing for childbirth and is impenetrable. This is characteristic of both male and female hyena, because of hyperactive abnormal sexuality; the male lies with the male so that it rarely approaches

138

the female. For that reason, births are infrequent among hyenas, because they so freely sow their seed contrary to nature. In the case of hyenas, nature, in her diversity, has added this additional organ to accomodate their excessive sexual activity. Therefore, it is large enough for the service of the lusting organs, but its opening is obstructed within. In short, it is not made to serve any purpose in generation.

St Clement of Alexandria from *The Instructor*
translated by Simon P. Wood

༈

PETRUCHIO
Come, come, you wasp; i'faith, you are too angry.

KATHARINA
If I be waspish, best beware my sting.

PETRUCHIO
My remedy is then, to pluck it out.

KATHARINA
Ay, if the fool could find it where it lies.

PETRUCHIO
Who knows not where a wasp does wear his sting? In his tail.

KATHARINA
In his tongue.

PETRUCHIO
Whose tongue?

KATHARINA
Yours, if you talk of tails: and so farewell.

PETRUCHIO

What, with my tongue in your tail? nay, come again,
Good Kate; I am a gentleman.

William Shakespeare from *The Taming of the Shrew*

∿

The sudden joy and strong surprise
Shook off the slumber from his eyes,
And strangely he began to stare,
To find his finger — *you know where.*

La Fontaine from *Les Cent Nouvelles Nouvelles*
translated by Mr Humphreys

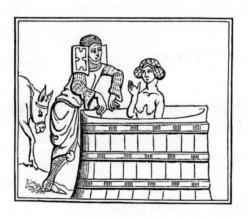

INDEX OF AUTHORS

INDEX